Collins · *do brilliantly !*

Test**Practice**

KS3 Maths

Test practice at its **best**

- **Kevin Evans**
- **Keith Gordon**
- **Series Editor: Jayne de Courcy**

William Collins' dream of knowledge for all began with the publication of his first book in 1819. A self-educated mill worker, he not only enriched millions of lives, but also founded a flourishing publishing house. Today, staying true to this spirit, Collins books are packed with inspiration, innovation and practical expertise. They place you at the centre of a world of possibility and give you exactly what you need to explore it.

Collins. Do more.

Published by Collins
An imprint of HarperCollins*Publishers*
77–85 Fulham Palace Road
Hammersmith
London
W6 8JB

Browse the complete Collins catalogue at
www.collinseducation.com

© HarperCollins*Publishers* Ltd 2005
This new edition published 2006

10 9 8 7 6 5 4 3

ISBN-13 978 0 00 721542 3
ISBN-10 0 00 721542 8

British Library Cataloguing in Publication Data
A catalogue record for this book is available from the British Library

Edited by Margaret Shepherd
Production by Katie Butler
Design by Bob Vickers and Gecko Limited
Printed and bound by Printing Express, Hong Kong

Illustrations
Jerry Fowler

You might also like to visit:
www.harpercollins.co.uk
The book lover's website

Contents

About the Maths National Test

When is the Test?

You will sit your Maths National Test in May of Year 9. Your teacher will give you the exact dates.

What does the Test cover?

The Maths curriculum is divided into four Attainment Targets. The Test covers all four of these:

Ma1 Using and Applying Mathematics
Ma2 Number and Algebra
Ma3 Shape, Space and Measures
Ma4 Handling Data

See the note on page vi about Using and Applying Mathematics.

How many papers are there?

You take two Test papers – Paper 1 and Paper 2 – and a Mental arithmetic test.

The Test papers are set at four different tiers:

The tiers overlap and some of the questions are the same across the overlapping tiers.

If you take the Tier 3–5 paper, you can achieve a level 3, 4 or 5. If you take the Tier 4–6 paper, you can achieve a level 4, 5 or 6, and so on. Everyone has to take a Test in one of these tiers. Your teacher will decide which tier will best allow you to show what you know and understand about Maths.

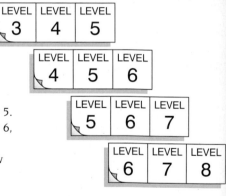

LEVEL	LEVEL	LEVEL
3	4	5

LEVEL	LEVEL	LEVEL
4	5	6

LEVEL	LEVEL	LEVEL
5	6	7

LEVEL	LEVEL	LEVEL
6	7	8

Can I use a calculator?

You can only use a calculator in Paper 2.

What is a good grade?

By the end of Key Stage 3, most pupils are between levels 3 and 7. A typical 14 year old will achieve a level 5 or 6 in their National Test.

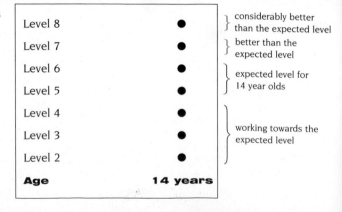

Level 8	●	} considerably better than the expected level
Level 7	●	} better than the expected level
Level 6	●	} expected level for 14 year olds
Level 5	●	
Level 4	●	
Level 3	●	} working towards the expected level
Level 2	●	
Age	**14 years**	

How this book can help boost your Test result

1 Practise the right tier – no Test surprises

This book contains a complete Paper 1 and a complete Paper 2 **at all four tiers**. It is clearly marked where each tier begins and ends.

Your teacher will tell you which tier you will be entered for. You can then work through the complete Paper 1 and Paper 2 for that tier.

2 Answers and Comments – to boost your grade

Detailed guidance is given in addition to the correct answer for each question.

This means that if you get an answer wrong, you will be able to see where you went wrong and learn what to do next time.

3 'Where to find more help' – inside help from the experts

The 'Where to find more help' section, gives you even more guidance. It tells you which chapter of **Collins Revision Guide KS3 Maths** will help you revise the topic thoroughly.

4 Practise for the Mental arithmetic test

This book contains two Mental arithmetic tests.
This is how the Mental tests need to be set:

- Find a friend or parent to read you the questions. (In the National Test the questions will be on a tape which your teacher will play to you.)
- Select the answer sheet from the back of this book. You will need to cut out the sheet or photocopy it.

- Work out all the answers in your head and write them in the boxes on the answer sheet.
- Each question will be read to you twice and you will be given a set amount of time to answer each question.

5 Practise working under Test conditions

- Choose somewhere quiet to work while you are doing the Test.
- Make sure you have everything you need: pen, pencil, rubber, ruler, protractor and calculator.
- In the Test you will be allowed 1 hour to complete each paper. To get used to working under timed conditions, don't spend more than 1 hour on each paper.

- Leave time to check your answers carefully within the 1 hour.
- Do Paper 1 and Paper 2 on separate days.

If you use this book properly, it will give you the best possible preparation for your actual Test – and help you achieve your best Test score.

How to calculate your level

To find out what level you have achieved, add up the marks you got on the Mental arithmetic test and Papers 1 and 2. Remember: you must do Mental arithmetic test C if you do the Tier 3–5 papers, and test A/B for the higher tier papers.

The table below shows you the marks for each level at each tier. (N means no level awarded.)

Level	Tier 3–5	Tier 4–6	Tier 5–7	Tier 6–8
N	0–27	0–23	0–25	0–32
2	28–33			
3	34–67	24–29		
4	68–101	30–54	26–31	
5	102+	55–82	32–53	33–38
6		83+	54–85	39–59
7			86+	60–96
8				97+

You might want to try papers at more than one tier. For example, if you did the Tier 3–5 papers and Mental arithmetic test C and scored more than 102 altogether, this means that you have achieved a level 5. You could then try the Tier 4–6 papers (and Mental arithmetic test A/B) to see if you can get a total of more than 83. If so, you would achieve a level 6. Your teacher will give you advice about which tier to enter in the actual Test.

A note about Understanding and Applying Mathematics questions

There are three ways that Understanding and Applying Mathematics can be tested.

1 Problem solving
This tests if you can sort out complex questions and use your Mathematics in unusual situations. Examples of this type of question are Paper 1 Questions 13 (page 8) and 16 (page 10) and Paper 2 Questions 9 (page 31) and 17 (page 36).

2 Communicating
This tests if you can explain your Mathematics and use appropriate language and symbols. Examples of this type of question are Paper 1 Questions 11(c) (page 7) and 29(b) (page 16) and Paper 2 Questions 6 (page 29) and 11(c) (page 33).

3 Reasoning
This tests if you can write solutions in a logical way and show or prove results. Examples of this type of question are Paper 1 Questions 9 (page 6), 12(a and b) (page 8) and 39(a and b) (page 24) and Paper 2 Questions 12(b) (page 33), 15(b) (page 35) and 16(b) (page 35).

Formulae

You might need to use these formulae.

Trapezium

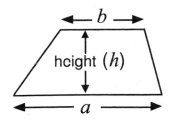

Area $= \frac{1}{2}(a + b)h$

Prism

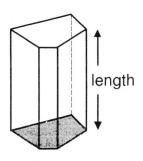

Volume $=$ area of cross-section $\times$ length

Instructions

Answers

This means: show your working and write down your answer.

Calculators

You **must not** use a calculator to answer any question in this test.

Calculators

You **may** use a calculator to answer any question in this test.

Paper 1

THIS IS THE START OF THE TIER 3–5 PAPER

1   (a)   Brian asked 32 pupils in his class if they stayed for school lunch.

20 pupils said '**Yes**'.
12 pupils said '**No**'.

Calculators

You **must not** use a calculator to answer any question in this test.

He draws a pictogram using the key ■ to represent 4 pupils.

Complete the pictogram to show his results.

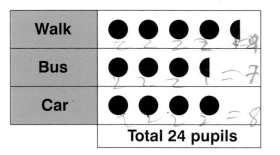

Yes	■ ■ ■ ■ ■
No	

Total 32 pupils

....
1 mark

(b)   Jill asked 24 pupils in her class how they usually travelled to school.

She also drew a pictogram using the key ● to represent 2 pupils.

Walk	● ● ● ● ●
Bus	● ● ● ●
Car	● ● ● ●

Total 24 pupils

How many pupils walked to school?

........9.......

....
1 mark

2   Write in the boxes what the missing numbers could be.

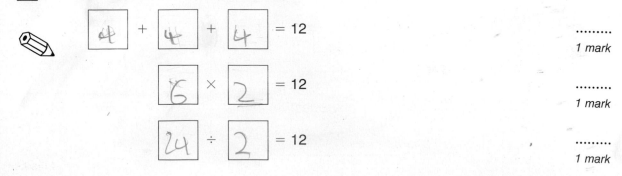

$$\boxed{4} + \boxed{4} + \boxed{4} = 12$$

....
1 mark

$$\boxed{6} \times \boxed{2} = 12$$

....
1 mark

$$\boxed{24} \div \boxed{2} = 12$$

....
1 mark

3 (a) Look at this scale.

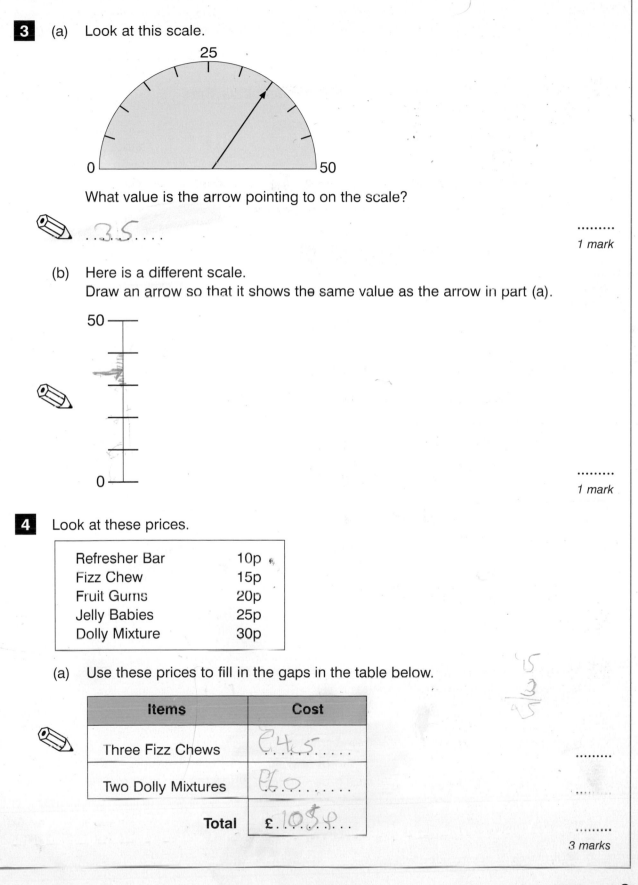

25

0   50

What value is the arrow pointing to on the scale?

..3.5....

....
1 mark

(b) Here is a different scale.
Draw an arrow so that it shows the same value as the arrow in part (a).

50 —

0 —

....
1 mark

4 Look at these prices.

Refresher Bar	10p
Fizz Chew	15p
Fruit Gums	20p
Jelly Babies	25p
Dolly Mixture	30p

(a) Use these prices to fill in the gaps in the table below.

Items	Cost
Three Fizz Chews	£45
Two Dolly Mixtures	£60
Total	£105p

....

....

....
3 marks

(b) There are different ways to make a total cost of 40p.
Use the prices to fill in the gaps below.
One is done for you.

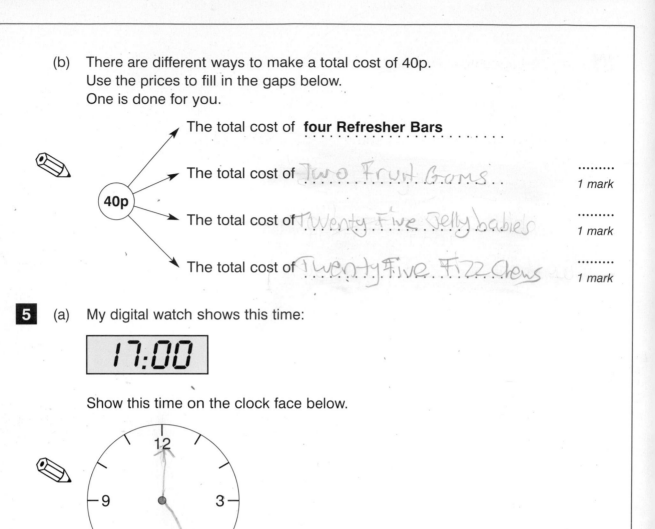

The total cost of **four Refresher Bars** . . . .

The total cost of *Two Fruit Gums* . .

.... *1 mark*

The total cost of *Twenty Five Jelly babies*

.... *1 mark*

The total cost of *Twenty Five Fizz chews*

.... *1 mark*

40p

5 (a) My digital watch shows this time:

17:00

Show this time on the clock face below.

(clock face showing 12, 9, 3, 6)

.... *1 mark*

(b) In the morning my digital watch shows this time:

07:50

What time is my digital watch showing one half-hour later?

:

.... *1 mark*

(c) My digital watch is a 24-hour watch.
A programme on TV starts at a quarter to eight in the evening.
What time will my digital watch be showing when the programme starts?

:

.... *1 mark*

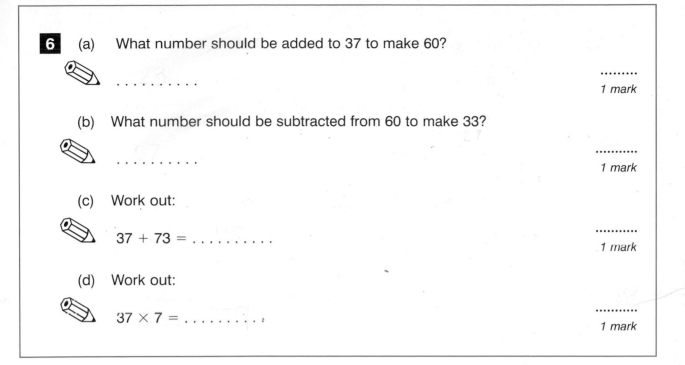

6 (a) What number should be added to 37 to make 60?

....

1 mark

(b) What number should be subtracted from 60 to make 33?

....

1 mark

(c) Work out:

37 + 73 = ...

1 mark

(d) Work out:

37 × 7 = ...

1 mark

> ◀ **THIS IS THE START OF THE TIER 4–6 PAPER**

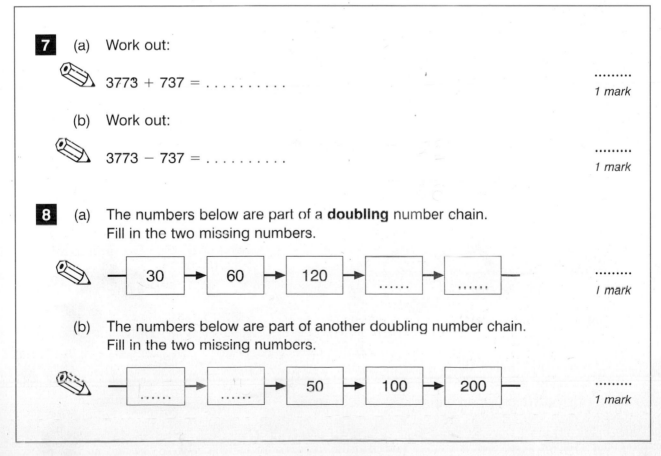

7 (a) Work out:

3773 + 737 = ...

1 mark

(b) Work out:

3773 − 737 = ...

1 mark

8 (a) The numbers below are part of a **doubling** number chain.
Fill in the two missing numbers.

| 30 | → | 60 | → | 120 | → | ...... | → | ...... |

....
1 mark

(b) The numbers below are part of another doubling number chain.
Fill in the two missing numbers.

| ...... | → | ...... | → | 50 | → | 100 | → | 200 |

....
1 mark

9 Trevor has five number cards.

Each card has a different whole number written on it.

If he takes a card at random, then

it is **certain** that the card will show a multiple of four, and

it is **impossible** that the card will show a number greater than 20.

What numbers are on the cards?

....

....

2 marks

10 The table below shows the increase in temperature during the day in four different towns.

Fill in the gaps in the table.

The first one has been done for you.

Town	Temperature at 6 am (°C)	Temperature at 3 pm (°C)	Increase in temperature (°C)
A	3	12	9
B	⁻3	5	....
C	⁻6	....	5
D	....	12	20

....
1 mark

....
1 mark

....
1 mark

11 Martha and Dylan are playing a game using two fair five-sided spinners as shown below.

Spinner A

Spinner B

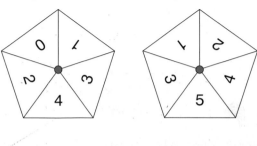

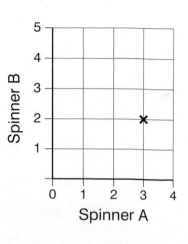

Martha goes first and scores 3 on spinner A and 2 on spinner B.

Her **total score** is 5.

She puts a cross on a grid to show her score.

(a) Dylan takes his turn.
     He has a **total score** of 7.

     Put crosses on the grid to show
     all the different possible pairs of
     numbers that Dylan's spinners
     could show.

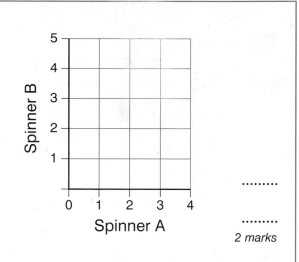

....

....

2 marks

(b) Martha has another turn and this
     time she gets the **same** number
     on both spinners.

     Put crosses on the grid to show
     all the different possible pairs of
     numbers that Martha's spinners
     could show.

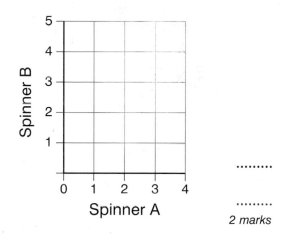

....

....

2 marks

(c) The grid shows the next four total
     scores in the game.
     Dylan says that he can spot a pattern.

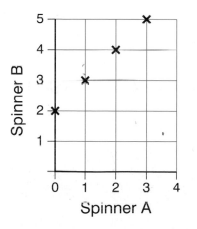

Complete the sentence below to describe Dylan's pattern.

The number on spinner B is always . . . .

. . . .

....

1 mark

12 Look at the two shapes on the grid.

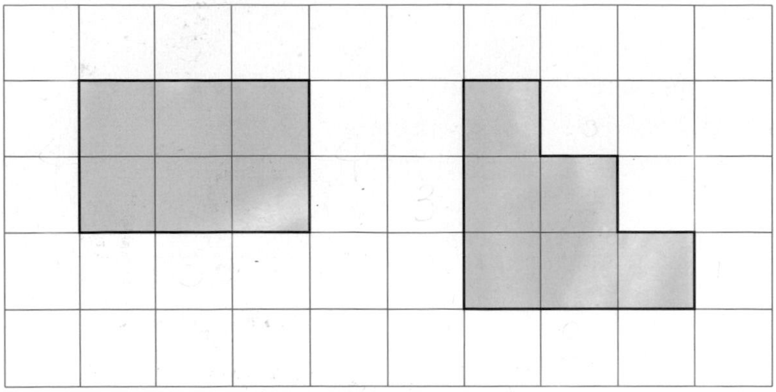

(a) Do the two shapes have the **same area**?
Tick (✔) Yes or No.

☐ Yes   ☐ No

Explain your answer.

....
1 mark

(b) Do the two shapes have the **same perimeter**?
Tick (✔) Yes or No.

☐ Yes   ☐ No

Explain your answer.

....
1 mark

13 Mark buys three bottles of wine from the supermarket.
The two large bottles have the same capacity.
The capacity of the small bottle is 0.7 litres.
The total capacity of the three bottles is 3.7 litres.

Find the capacity of one large bottle.

. . . . litres

....
....
2 marks

14 Linda has four identical squares.

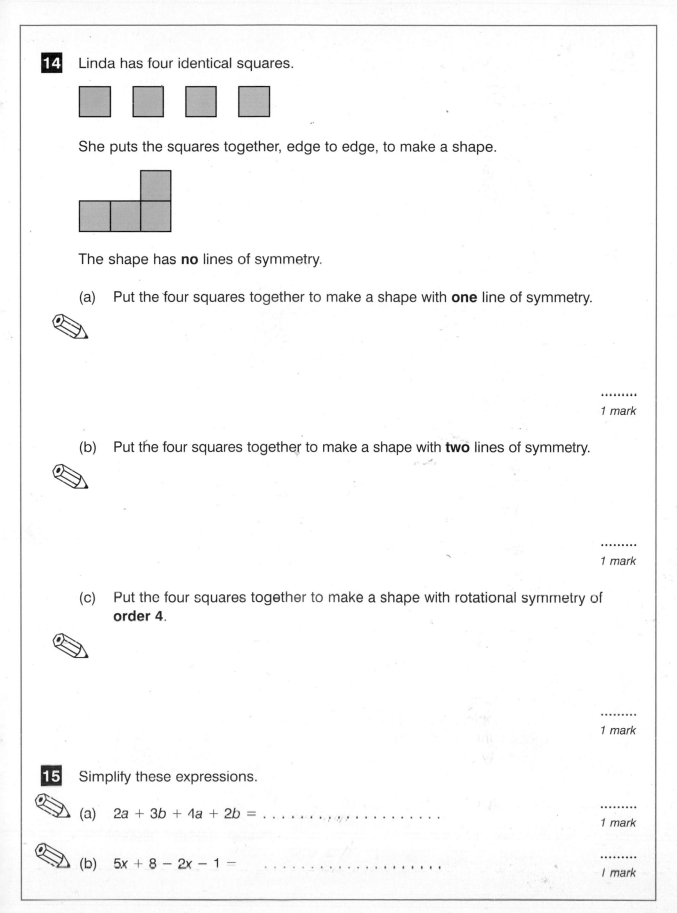

She puts the squares together, edge to edge, to make a shape.

The shape has **no** lines of symmetry.

(a)   Put the four squares together to make a shape with **one** line of symmetry.

....
1 mark

(b)   Put the four squares together to make a shape with **two** lines of symmetry.

....
1 mark

(c)   Put the four squares together to make a shape with rotational symmetry of **order 4**.

....
1 mark

15 Simplify these expressions.

(a) $2a + 3b + 4a + 2b =$ . . . .
....
1 mark

(b) $5x + 8 - 2x - 1 =$ . . . .
....
1 mark

THIS IS THE START OF THE TIER 5–7 PAPER

16 A drinks vending machine in a canteen shows this sign.

All drinks 30p

Only use these coins

5p   10p   20p

No change given

Complete the table to show all the different ways of paying **exactly 30p**.

Number of 5p coins	Number of 10p coins	Number of 20p coins
6	0	0

....

....

2 marks

17 Fill in the missing numbers.

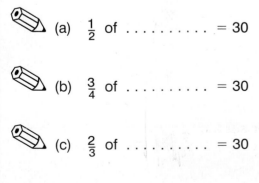

(a) $\frac{1}{2}$ of . . . . = 30

....

1 mark

(b) $\frac{3}{4}$ of . . . . = 30

....

1 mark

(c) $\frac{2}{3}$ of . . . . = 30

....

1 mark

18   Triangle ABC is moved on this square grid.

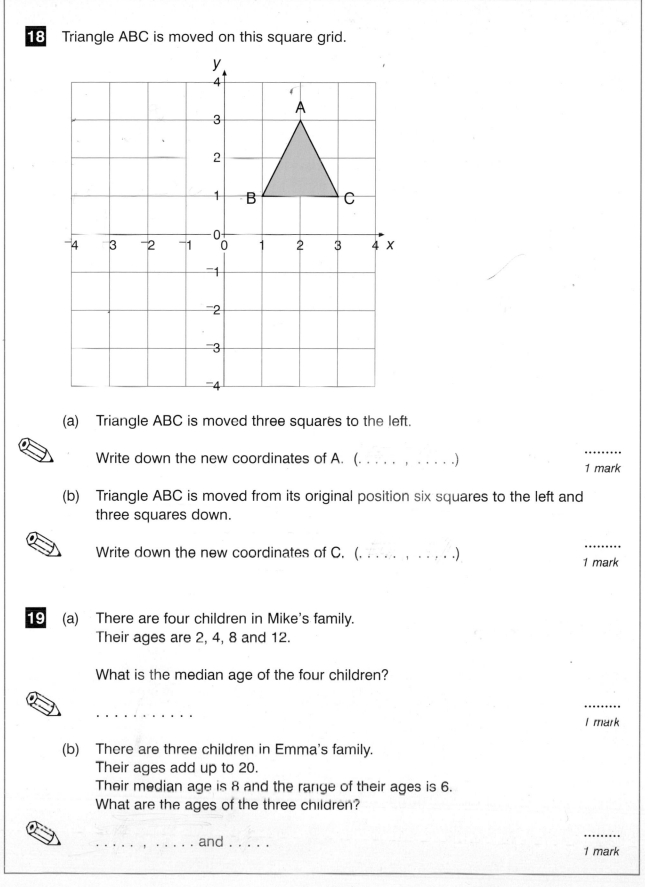

(a)   Triangle ABC is moved three squares to the left.

Write down the new coordinates of A.   (. . . . . , ...)

....
1 mark

(b)   Triangle ABC is moved from its original position six squares to the left and three squares down.

Write down the new coordinates of C.   (. . . . . , ...)

....
1 mark

19   (a)   There are four children in Mike's family.
Their ages are 2, 4, 8 and 12.

What is the median age of the four children?

. . . .

....
1 mark

(b)   There are three children in Emma's family.
Their ages add up to 20.
Their median age is 8 and the range of their ages is 6.
What are the ages of the three children?

. . . . . , ... and . . . . .

....
1 mark

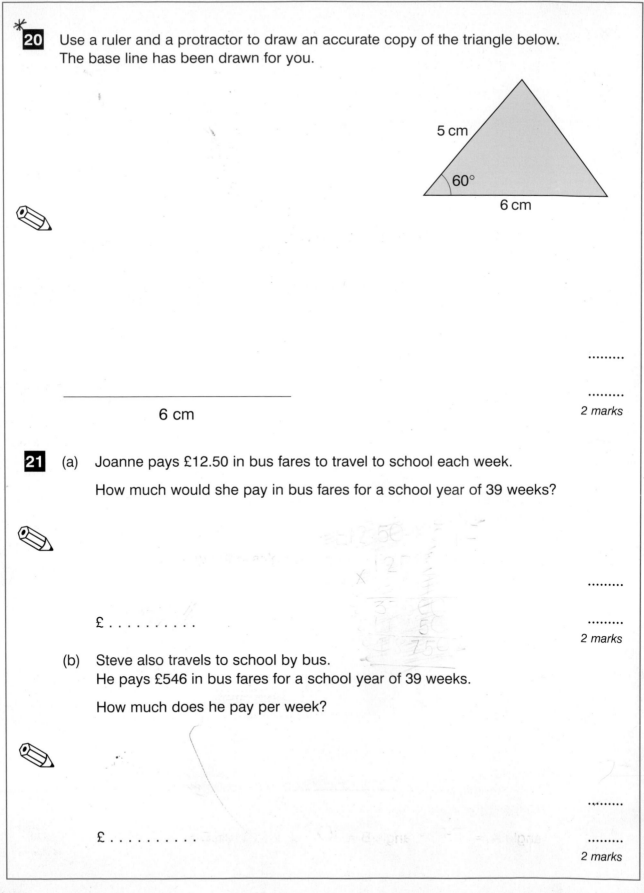

20 Use a ruler and a protractor to draw an accurate copy of the triangle below. The base line has been drawn for you.

5 cm

60°

6 cm

6 cm

....

....

2 marks

21 (a) Joanne pays £12.50 in bus fares to travel to school each week.

How much would she pay in bus fares for a school year of 39 weeks?

....

£ . . . .

....

2 marks

(b) Steve also travels to school by bus.
He pays £546 in bus fares for a school year of 39 weeks.

How much does he pay per week?

....

£ . . . .

....

2 marks

22   Solve these equations.

(a) $4a + 3 = 23$

$a = \ldots\ldots\ldots\ldots$

....
1 mark

(b) $2b - 1 = 4$

$b = \ldots\ldots\ldots\ldots$

....
1 mark

THIS IS THE END OF THE TIER 3–5 PAPER

THIS IS THE START OF THE TIER 6–8 PAPER

23   Solve these equations.

(a) $5x - 6 = 3x + 1$

....

$x = \ldots\ldots\ldots\ldots$

....
2 marks

(b) $3(2y + 5) = 3$

....

$y = \ldots\ldots\ldots\ldots$

....
2 marks

24   Work out the size of each of the unknown angles in the quadrilateral ABCD below.

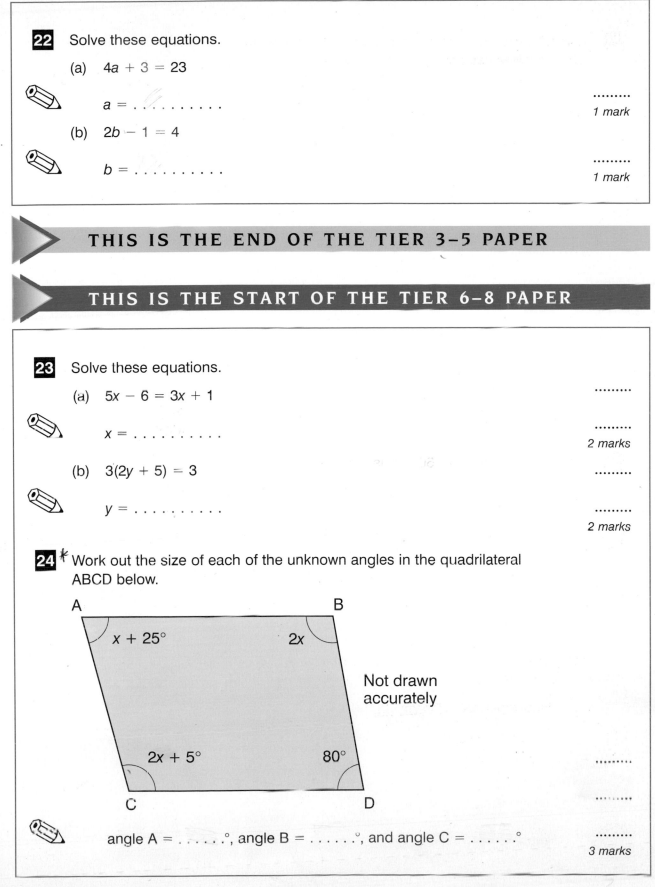

Not drawn accurately

angle A = ...°, angle B = ...°, and angle C = ...°

....
3 marks

25 (a) Add $\frac{7}{10}$ and $\frac{9}{10}$.

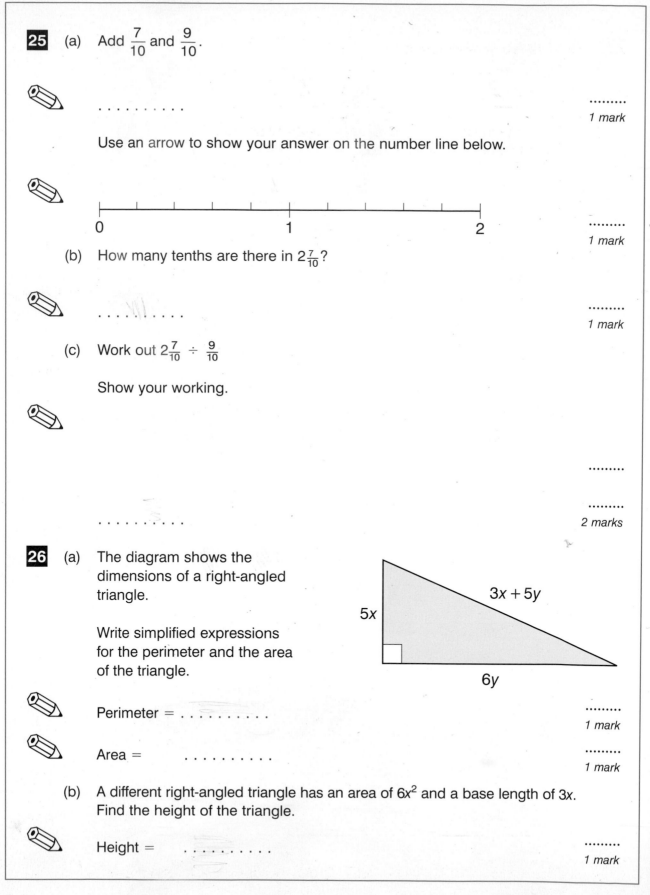

. . . .

.... *1 mark*

Use an arrow to show your answer on the number line below.

.... *1 mark*

(b) How many tenths are there in $2\frac{7}{10}$?

. . . .

.... *1 mark*

(c) Work out $2\frac{7}{10} \div \frac{9}{10}$

Show your working.

....

. . . .

.... *2 marks*

26 (a) The diagram shows the dimensions of a right-angled triangle.

Write simplified expressions for the perimeter and the area of the triangle.

Perimeter = ...

.... *1 mark*

Area = ...

.... *1 mark*

(b) A different right-angled triangle has an area of $6x^2$ and a base length of $3x$. Find the height of the triangle.

Height = ...

.... *1 mark*

27 Here are five number cards.

| **1** | **2** | **3** | **4** | **5** |

(a) Arrange these five cards to make the calculations below.
The first one is done for you.

$7245 =$ **3** **4** **5** $\times$ **2** **1**

$3510 =$ **2** ▢ ▢ $\times$ ▢ **5**   ....
                                                    1 mark

$7874 =$ ▢ ▢ **4** $\times$ **3** ▢   ....
                                                    1 mark

(b) Now arrange the five cards to complete the calculation below.

$5940 \div$ ▢ ▢ ▢ $=$ **4** **5**   ....
                                                    1 mark

28 The diagram shows a rectangle ABCD drawn on a square grid.

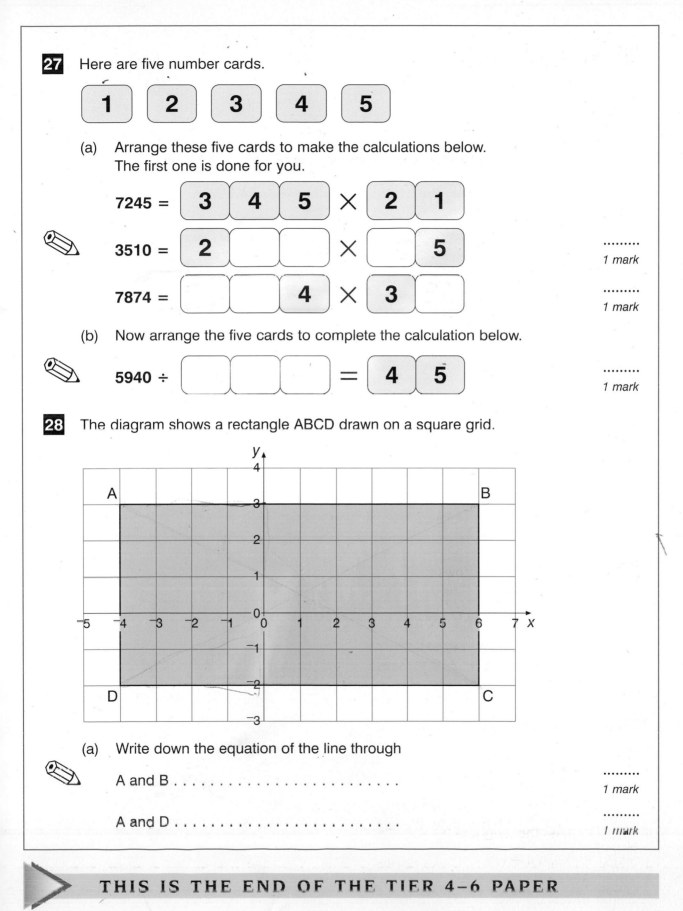

(a) Write down the equation of the line through

A and B . . . .
                                                    1 mark

A and D . . . .
                                                    1 mark

THIS IS THE END OF THE TIER 4–6 PAPER

(b) AC and BD are the diagonals of the rectangle.
     Draw arrows to match each diagonal to the correct equation for the line.

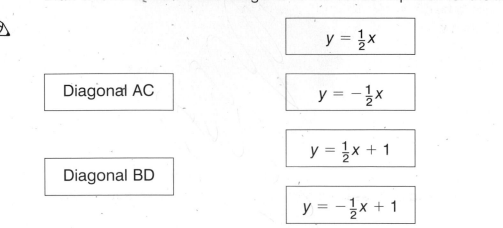

| Diagonal AC |

$$y = \tfrac{1}{2}x$$

$$y = -\tfrac{1}{2}x$$

$$y = \tfrac{1}{2}x + 1$$

| Diagonal BD |

$$y = -\tfrac{1}{2}x + 1$$

....

....

2 marks

29 The table shows the heights and masses of 12 athletes.

Height (cm)	155	156	157	158	159	160	164	165	167	173	180	185
Mass (kg)	58	60	60	61	58	63	66	63	62	66	69	72

(a) Show this information on a scatter graph on the grid below.

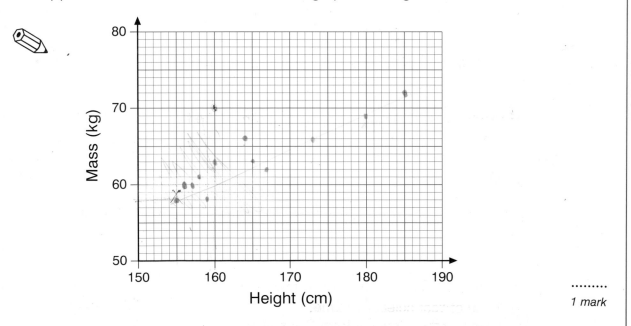

....
1 mark

(b) Describe what the scatter graph shows about the relationship between the
     height of an athlete and the mass of an athlete.

     Shows tendence to increase with some outsiders

....
1 mark

(c)   Draw a line of best fit on the scatter graph.

....
1 mark

(d)   Terry's height is 160 cm and his mass is 70 kg.
        Explain why Terry is not likely to be an athlete.

He is really out of the scatter graph

....
1 mark

30   A gift voucher is to be presented to a pupil who has had full attendance
        for a term.
        The table shows the number of pupils who have had full attendance in
        three classes.

Class	Number of boys	Number of girls
9HW	7	8
9KE	6	8
9RH	9	5

The names of all these pupils are put into a bag and the Head of Year
selects one at random in an assembly.

(a)   What is the probability that the pupil chosen will be from Class 9KE?

....
1 mark

(b)   What is the probability that the pupil chosen will be a girl from Class 9HW?

....
1 mark

(c)   The Head of Year selects a name.
        She says that the winner is from Class 9RH.
        What is the probability that the winner is a boy?

....
1 mark

31 The diagram shows the distance Douglas travels on a motorway between Town A and Town B.
He stops for a break at a service station at C.
The diagram also shows the time it takes him to travel from Town A to the service station and the time it takes him to travel from the service station to Town B.

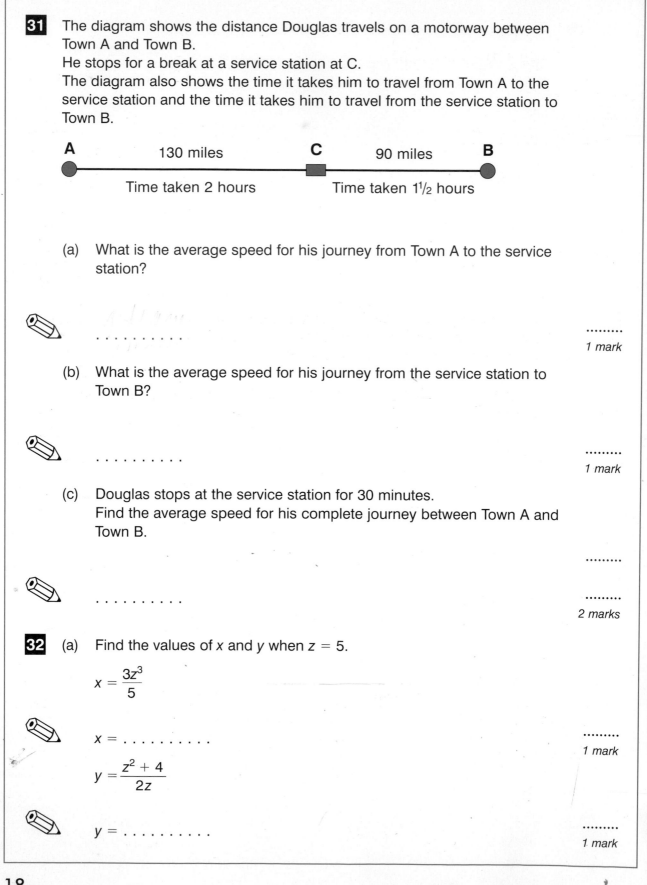

A   130 miles   C   90 miles   B

Time taken 2 hours   Time taken 1½ hours

(a) What is the average speed for his journey from Town A to the service station?

....

....
1 mark

(b) What is the average speed for his journey from the service station to Town B?

....

....
1 mark

(c) Douglas stops at the service station for 30 minutes.
Find the average speed for his complete journey between Town A and Town B.

....

....

....
2 marks

32 (a) Find the values of x and y when z = 5.

$$x = \frac{3z^3}{5}$$

$x = $ ....
1 mark

$$y = \frac{z^2 + 4}{2z}$$

$y = $ ....
1 mark

(b)   Multiply out and simplify these expressions.

$3(2p + 1) - 2(3 + 2p)$

. . . .

.... 1 mark

$s(s + 3) + 3(s^2 - 2)$

....

. . . .

.... 2 marks

33 The **scale diagram** below shows two radar stations X and Y.
The radar station at X has a range of 120 km.
The radar station at Y has a range of 100 km.
The direct distance between X and Y is 160 km.
On the diagram, show the region where an aircraft can be picked up by both radar stations.

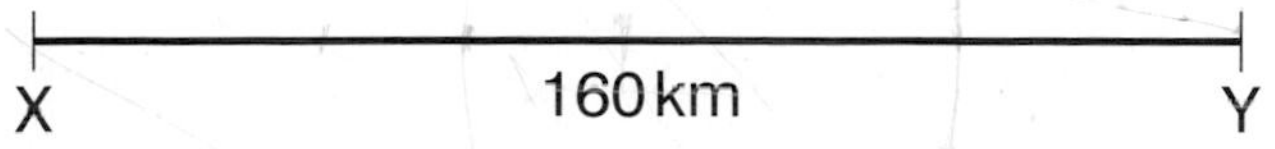

X   160 km   Y

....

.... 2 marks

34 (a) x is an even number.

Show that $(x - 1)(x + 1)$ is an odd number.

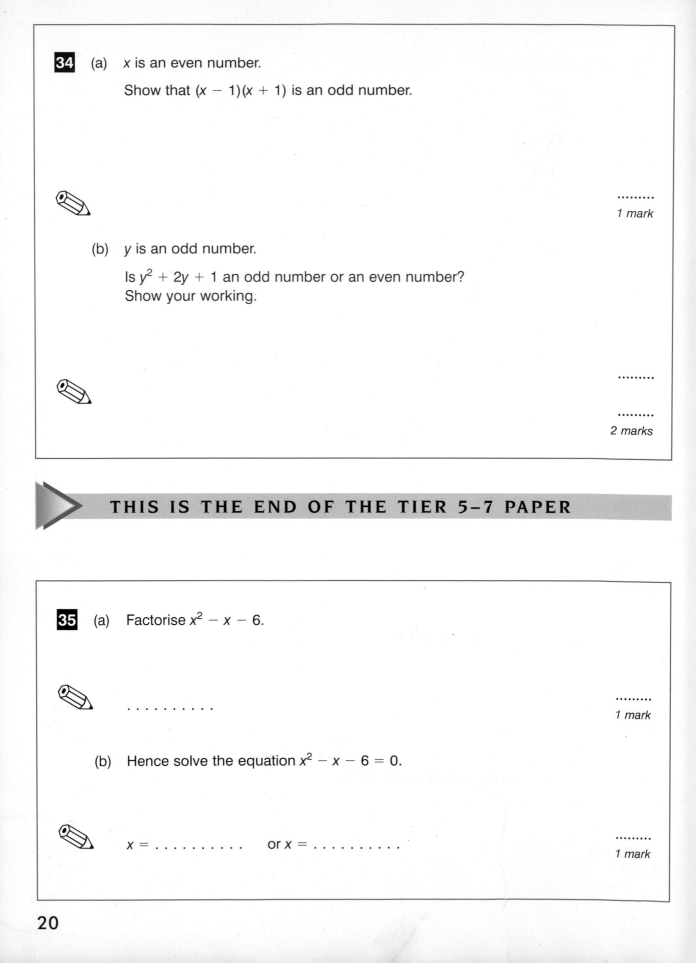

....
1 mark

(b) y is an odd number.

Is $y^2 + 2y + 1$ an odd number or an even number?
Show your working.

....

....
2 marks

THIS IS THE END OF THE TIER 5–7 PAPER

35 (a) Factorise $x^2 - x - 6$.

. . . .
....
1 mark

(b) Hence solve the equation $x^2 - x - 6 = 0$.

$x = $ . . . .   or $x = $ . . . .
....
1 mark

36 Look at this graph.

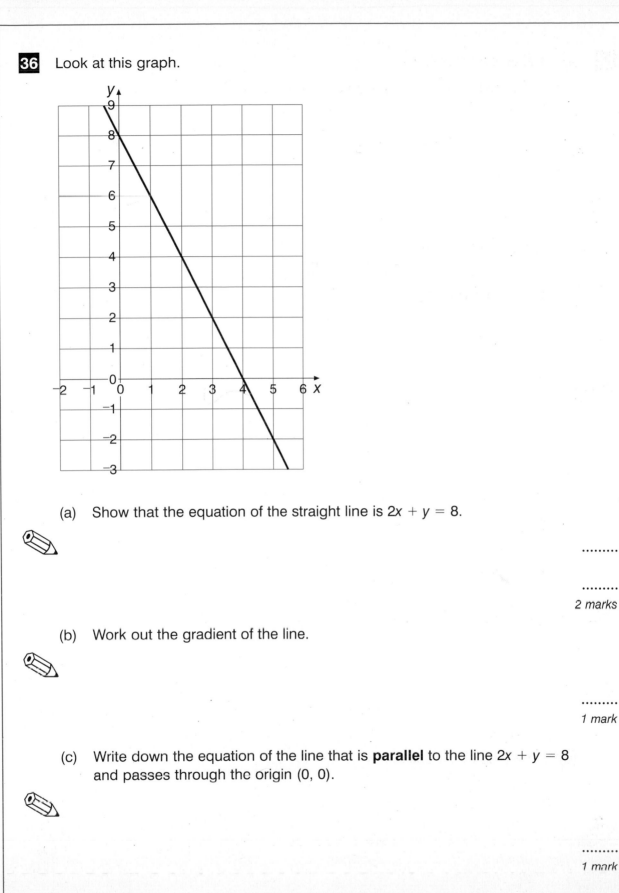

(a) Show that the equation of the straight line is $2x + y = 8$.

....

....

2 marks

(b) Work out the gradient of the line.

....

1 mark

(c) Write down the equation of the line that is **parallel** to the line $2x + y = 8$ and passes through the origin (0, 0).

....

1 mark

37 Mrs Saville asks 32 pupils in her class to estimate one minute.
She records their estimates in a cumulative frequency table as shown below.

Time (seconds)	Frequency	Cumulative frequency
$20 < x \leq 30$	1	
$30 < x \leq 40$	3	
$40 < x \leq 50$	7	
$50 < x \leq 60$	12	
$60 < x \leq 70$	4	
$70 < x \leq 80$	3	
$80 < x \leq 90$	2	

(a) Complete the cumulative frequency column.

....
1 mark

(b) Draw the cumulative frequency graph to show her results.

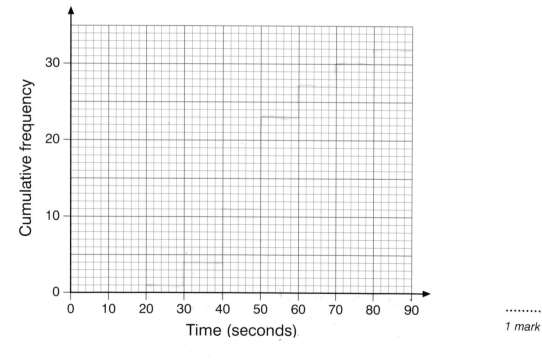

....
1 mark

(c) Use the graph to estimate the **median** time.

Median = ... seconds

....
1 mark

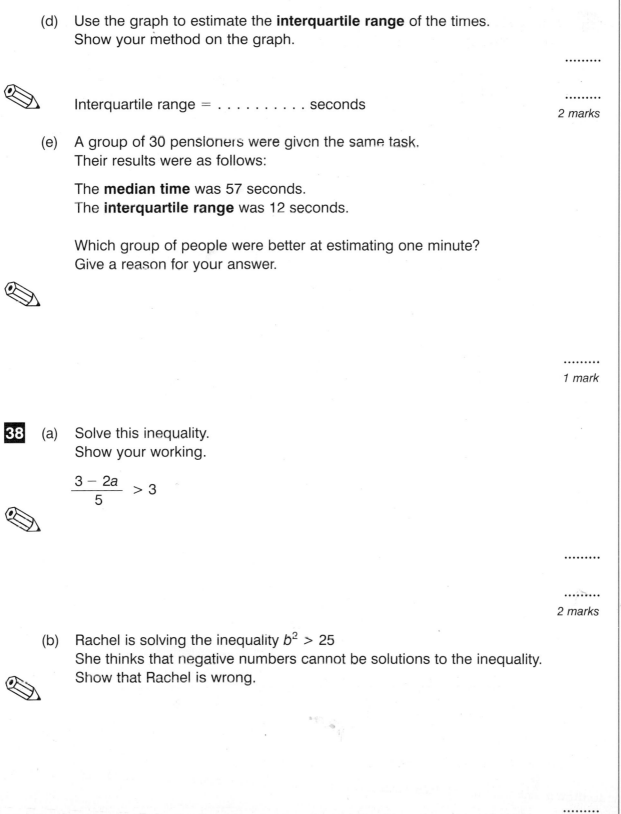

(d) Use the graph to estimate the **interquartile range** of the times.
     Show your method on the graph.

     ....

     Interquartile range = ... seconds   ....

                                                              2 marks

(e) A group of 30 pensioners were given the same task.
     Their results were as follows:

     The **median time** was 57 seconds.
     The **interquartile range** was 12 seconds.

     Which group of people were better at estimating one minute?
     Give a reason for your answer.

                                                              ....

                                                              1 mark

38 (a) Solve this inequality.
            Show your working.

            $$\frac{3 - 2a}{5} > 3$$

                                                              ....

                                                              ....

                                                              2 marks

     (b) Rachel is solving the inequality $b^2 > 25$
          She thinks that negative numbers cannot be solutions to the inequality.
          Show that Rachel is wrong.

                                                              ....

                                                              1 mark

39 The diagram shows three points X, Y and Z on the circumference of a circle with centre at O.
YZ is a diameter of the circle.

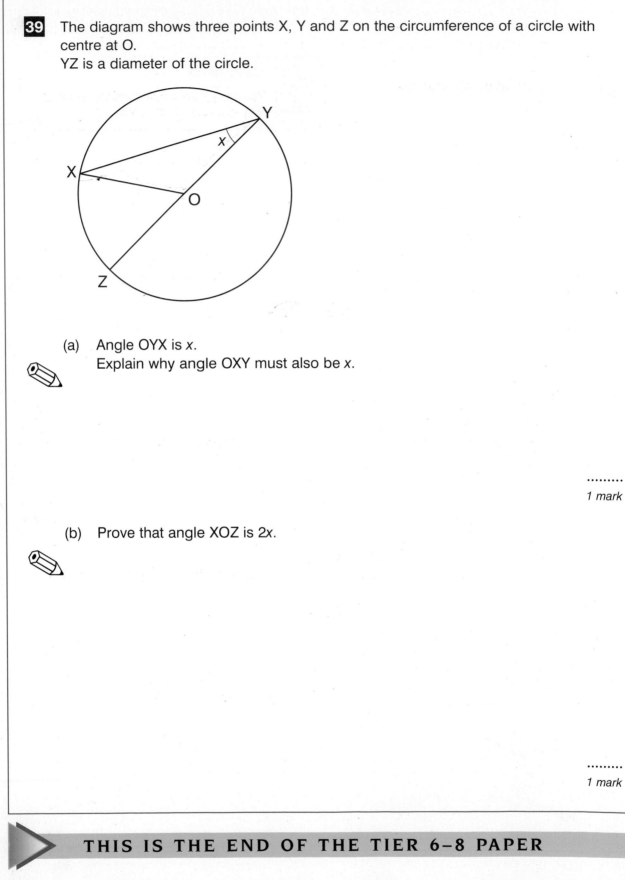

(a) Angle OYX is x.
Explain why angle OXY must also be x.

....
1 mark

(b) Prove that angle XOZ is $2x$.

....
1 mark

THIS IS THE END OF THE TIER 6–8 PAPER

Paper 2

1   (a)   Look at these shapes.

Calculators

You **may** use a calculator to answer any question in this test.

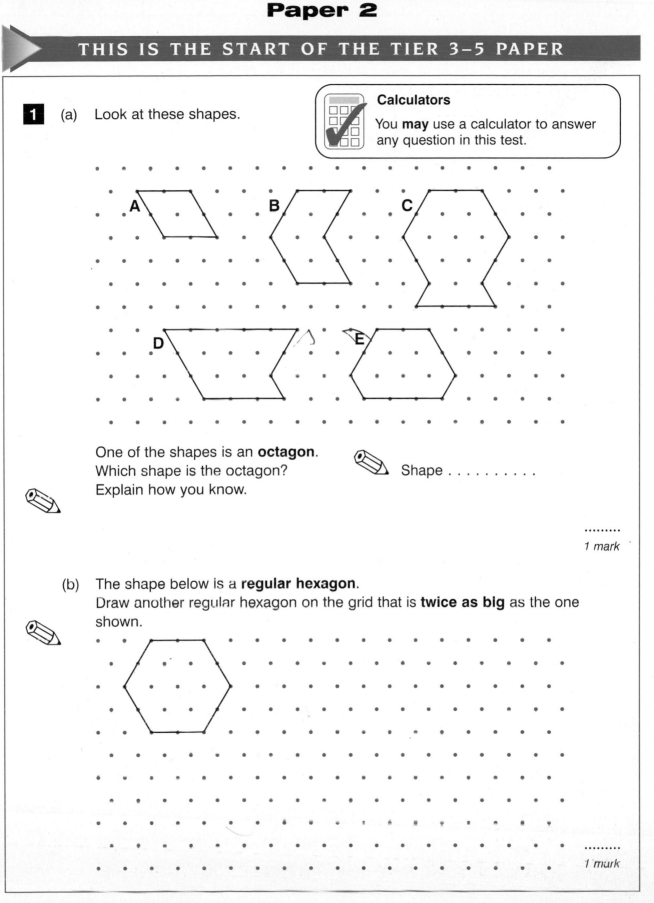

One of the shapes is an **octagon**.
Which shape is the octagon?
Explain how you know.

Shape . . . .

. . . .
1 mark

(b)   The shape below is a **regular hexagon**.
Draw another regular hexagon on the grid that is **twice as big** as the one shown.

. . . .
1 mark

25

2 Look at this diagram.
It shows the distances in metres between some attractions in the local park.

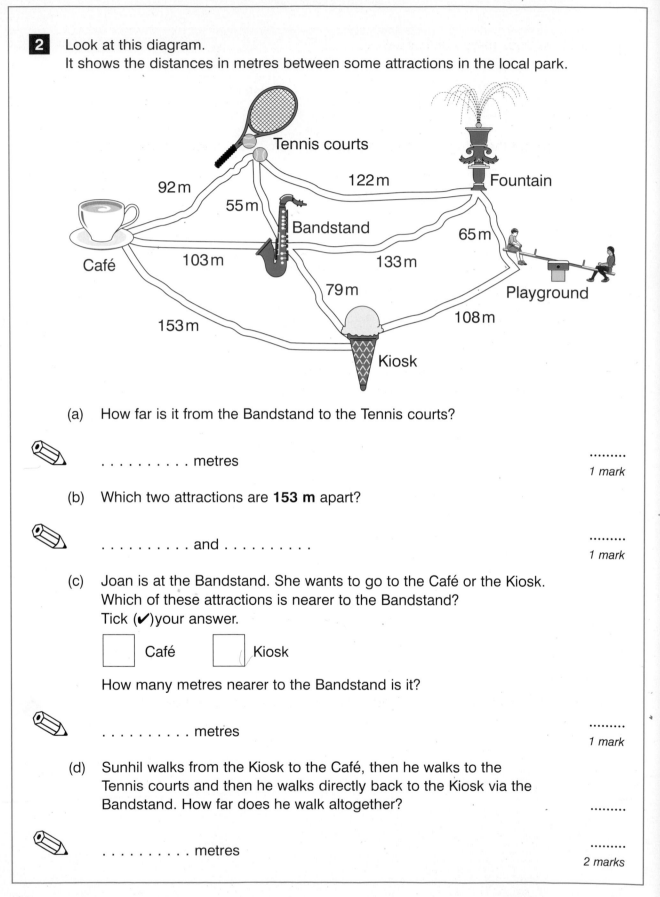

(a) How far is it from the Bandstand to the Tennis courts?

. . . . metres

.... *1 mark*

(b) Which two attractions are **153 m** apart?

. . . . and . . . .

.... *1 mark*

(c) Joan is at the Bandstand. She wants to go to the Café or the Kiosk.
Which of these attractions is nearer to the Bandstand?
Tick (✔)your answer.

☐ Café   ☐ Kiosk

How many metres nearer to the Bandstand is it?

. . . . metres

.... *1 mark*

(d) Sunhil walks from the Kiosk to the Café, then he walks to the
Tennis courts and then he walks directly back to the Kiosk via the
Bandstand. How far does he walk altogether?

. . . . metres

.... *2 marks*

3 Look at these three number cards.

| 0 | 6 | 3 |

You can put them together to show different numbers, for example:

| 0 | 3 | 6 | **Thirty six** . . . .

(a)   Put the cards together in a different way.
      Write in words what number the cards show.

| | 0 | | 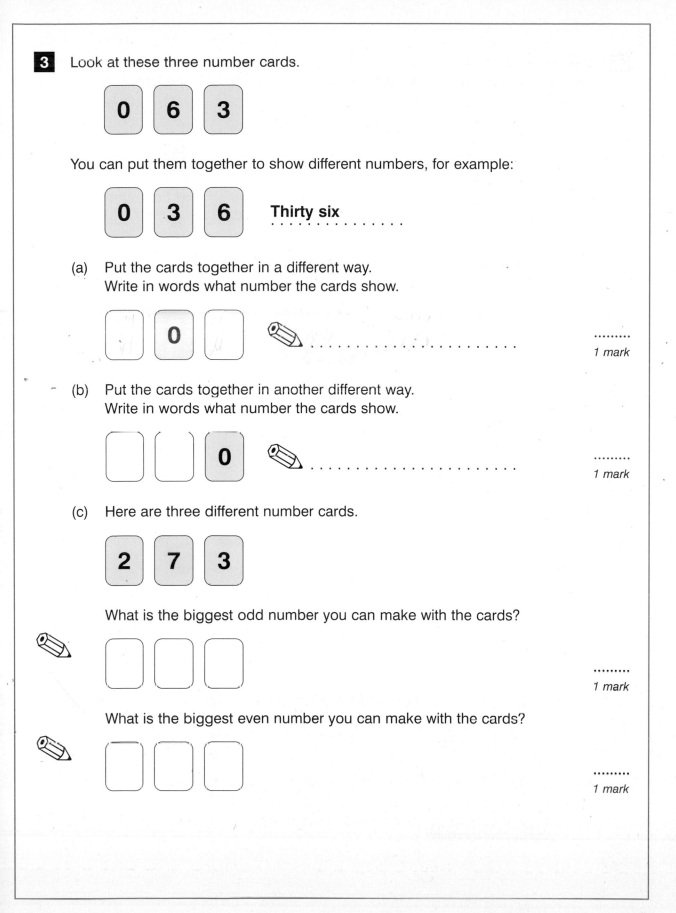 . . . .

....
1 mark

(b)   Put the cards together in another different way.
      Write in words what number the cards show.

| | | 0 | ✎ . . . .

....
1 mark

(c)   Here are three different number cards.

| 2 | 7 | 3 |

What is the biggest odd number you can make with the cards?

✎ | | | |

....
1 mark

What is the biggest even number you can make with the cards?

✎ | | | |

....
1 mark

4   A headmaster records the Key Stage 2 Maths National Tests results for three classes. The bar charts show the results.

Form 6A

Form 6B

Form 6C

(a)   **Altogether**, how many pupils got a Level 2 in the National Tests?

. . . . pupils

1 mark

(b)   **Altogether**, how many pupils are in Class 6B?

. . . . pupils

1 mark

(c)   One class attended extra lessons in Mathematics. Which class do you think that was?

Class . . . .

Explain why you made your choice.

. . . .

1 mark

5   (a)   How many **faces** does a **triangular prism** have?

. . . .

1 mark

(b)   How many **vertices** does a **cuboid** have?

. . . .

1 mark

(c) The top of a square-based pyramid is cut off to leave a **frustum**.
     How many faces does the frustum have?

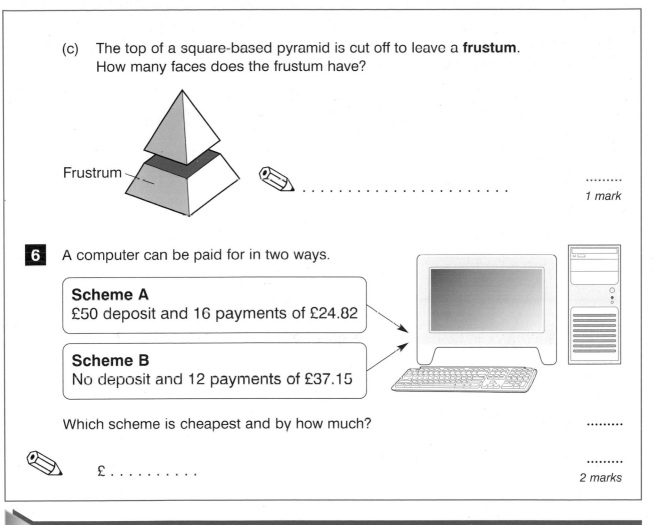

Frustrum

....

. . . .

1 mark

6 A computer can be paid for in two ways.

Scheme A
£50 deposit and 16 payments of £24.82

Scheme B
No deposit and 12 payments of £37.15

Which scheme is cheapest and by how much?

....

£ . . . .

....
2 marks

THIS IS THE START OF THE TIER 4–6 PAPER

7 Matthew did a survey. He asked pupils if they wanted to have a shorter lunch-hour?
     The table shows the results.

	Yes	No	Don't know
Boys	54	27	12
Girls	63	18	9

(a) How many **boys** took part in the survey?

. . . . . 93 . . . . . pupils

....
1 mark

(b) More pupils said '**Yes**' than said '**No**'. How many more?

. . . . pupils

....
1 mark

(c)   Matthew asked the same question of sixty staff. 60% said 'Yes', 25% said
      'No' and the rest said 'Don't know'.
      Complete the table to show the numbers of teachers that gave each
      answer.

	Yes	No	Don't know
Teachers			

....

....

2 marks

(d)   Emily did a further survey to find out if pupils in different years are in favour
      of a shorter lunch-hour.
      She decides to survey pupils in Years 7, 8 and 9.
      She asks them, 'What year are you in?'
              and 'Do you want a shorter lunch-hour?'
      Fill in the labels for the two-way table below so that Emily can record her
      results.

....			
....			

....

1 mark

8   The chart shows the number of years served and the age at which they started
       in the post for all the Prime Ministers since
       the Second World War (1945).

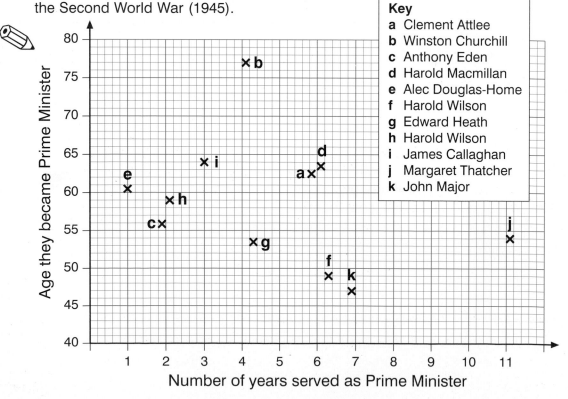

Key
a Clement Attlee
b Winston Churchill
c Anthony Eden
d Harold Macmillan
e Alec Douglas-Home
f Harold Wilson
g Edward Heath
h Harold Wilson
i James Callaghan
j Margaret Thatcher
k John Major

Use the chart to answer these questions.

(a)   For how many years did **James Callaghan** serve as Prime Minister?

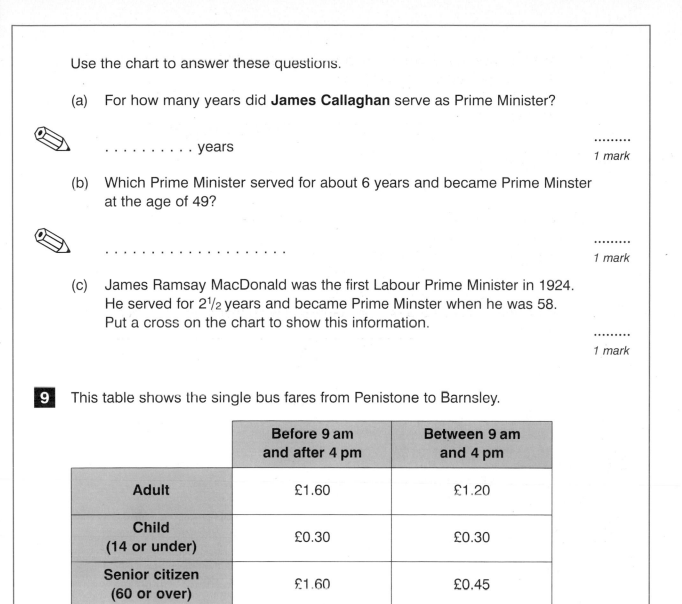

        . . . . years

....
1 mark

(b)   Which Prime Minister served for about 6 years and became Prime Minster at the age of 49?

        . . . .

....
1 mark

(c)   James Ramsay MacDonald was the first Labour Prime Minister in 1924. He served for 2$\frac{1}{2}$ years and became Prime Minster when he was 58. Put a cross on the chart to show this information.

....
1 mark

9   This table shows the single bus fares from Penistone to Barnsley.

	Before 9 am and after 4 pm	Between 9 am and 4 pm
Adult	£1.60	£1.20
Child (14 or under)	£0.30	£0.30
Senior citizen (60 or over)	£1.60	£0.45

The Smith family of Dad (aged 42), Mum (aged 40), Charles (aged 12), Shone (aged 16) and Grandad (aged 66) travel to Barnsley from Penistone at 10 am but come back at 7 pm.
How much did the journey cost them?

....

....

....
3 marks

10 A digital thermometer measures the temperature indoors and outside.

    (a) At 9 am the display shows:

| OUTSIDE 12.7°C |
| INSIDE   18.6°C |

        How much hotter is it inside than outside?

        . . . . °C

        1 mark

    (b) At 10 am the temperature outside has risen by 2.8 °C.
        What is the temperature outside at 10 am?

        . . . . °C

        1 mark

    (c) The thermometer can be set to measure in °C or °F.
        An approximate rule for converting from °C to °F is to double the
        temperature in °C and add 30.

        °C → ×2 → +30 → °F

        The least temperature the digital thermometer has recorded is ⁻10.4°C.
        Use the rule above to convert this temperature to °F.

        | °F |

        2 marks

11 In this question all the grids represent centimetre square grids.

    (a) Draw a rectangle that has a perimeter of 20 cm.

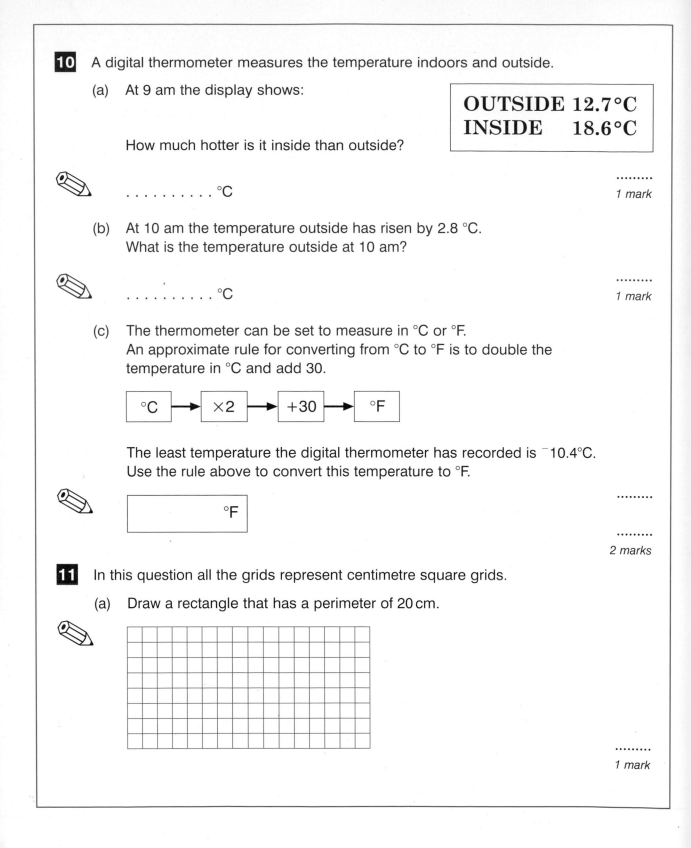

        1 mark

THIS IS THE START OF THE TIER 5–7 PAPER

(b) Draw another rectangle with a perimeter of 20 cm. This rectangle must have a different area from the rectangle in part (a).

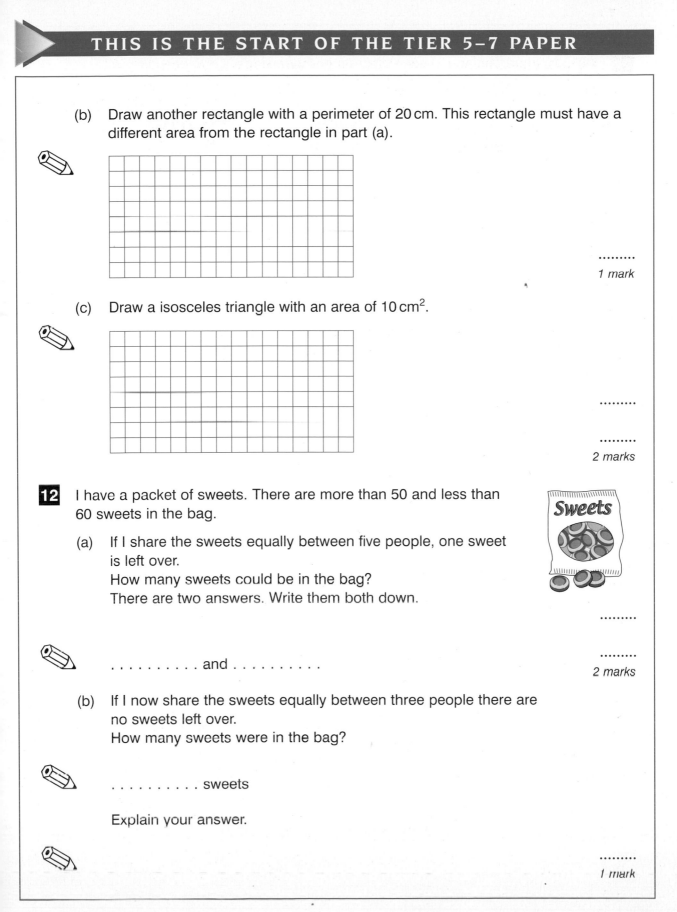

....
1 mark

(c) Draw a isosceles triangle with an area of 10 cm².

....

....
2 marks

12 I have a packet of sweets. There are more than 50 and less than 60 sweets in the bag.

(a) If I share the sweets equally between five people, one sweet is left over.
How many sweets could be in the bag?
There are two answers. Write them both down.

....

. . . . and . . . .

....
2 marks

(b) If I now share the sweets equally between three people there are no sweets left over.
How many sweets were in the bag?

. . . . sweets

Explain your answer.

....
1 mark

13 (a)   What percentage of each diagram is shaded?
The first one is done for you.

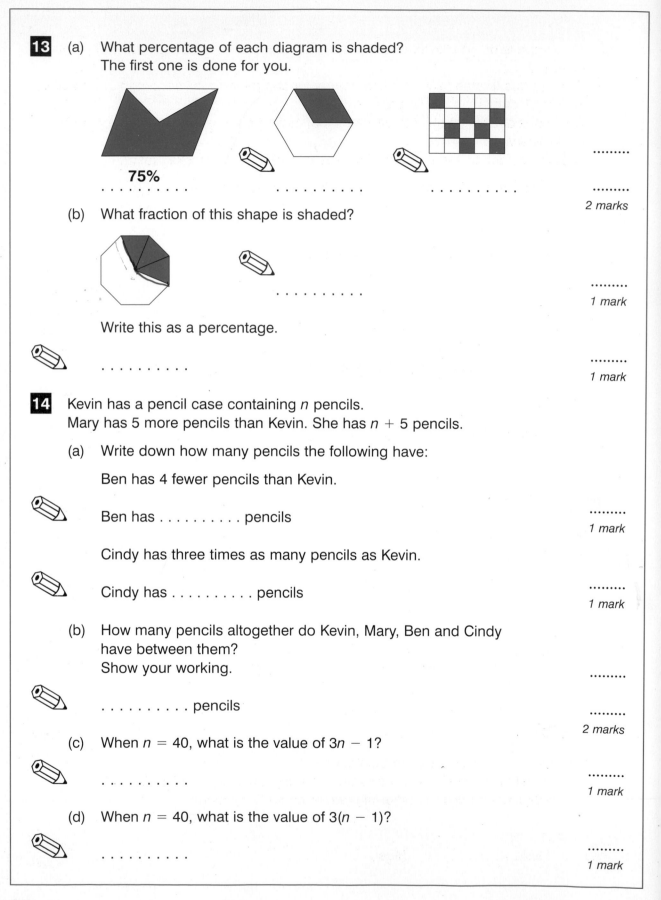

75%
. . . .

....
2 marks

(b)   What fraction of this shape is shaded?

. . . .
1 mark

Write this as a percentage.

. . . .
1 mark

14   Kevin has a pencil case containing n pencils.
Mary has 5 more pencils than Kevin. She has $n + 5$ pencils.

(a)   Write down how many pencils the following have:

Ben has 4 fewer pencils than Kevin.

Ben has . . . . pencils   ....
1 mark

Cindy has three times as many pencils as Kevin.

Cindy has . . . . pencils   ....
1 mark

(b)   How many pencils altogether do Kevin, Mary, Ben and Cindy
have between them?
Show your working.   ....

. . . . pencils
....
2 marks

(c)   When $n = 40$, what is the value of $3n - 1$?

. . . .
1 mark

(d)   When $n = 40$, what is the value of $3(n - 1)$?

. . . .
1 mark

15 Three pupils decide to conduct a survey about lunch-time eating habits of pupils in Year 7.
Asif decides to stand by the canteen one lunch-time and collect data from the first 30 Year 7 pupils that come past.
Benjy decides to get a list of all Year 7 pupils and choose every fifth name on the list to interview.
Cassie decides to ask the rest of her team-mates on the hockey team.

(a)   Choose a pupil whose survey will not give reliable data.

Pupil . . . .

Explain why the method is not a good one.

. . . .
1 mark

(b)   Which pupil's survey will give reliable data?

Pupil . . . .

Explain why the method is a good one.

. . . .
1 mark

16   (a)   Dennis has five counters. Three are red and two are white.

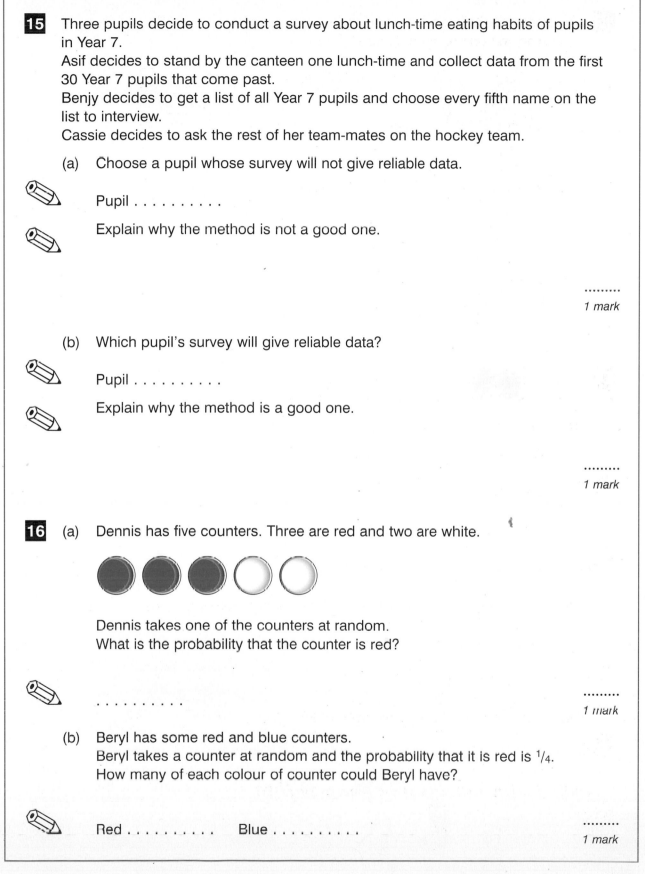

Dennis takes one of the counters at random.
What is the probability that the counter is red?

. . . .
. . . .
1 mark

(b)   Beryl has some red and blue counters.
Beryl takes a counter at random and the probability that it is red is $^1/_4$.
How many of each colour of counter could Beryl have?

Red . . . .   Blue . . . .
. . . .
1 mark

17 Look at the diagram. ABCD is an isosceles trapezium, with sides of 5 cm, 5 cm, 5 cm and 10 cm as shown.
ABCD is reflected in AB to give the diagram below.

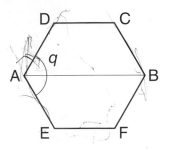

Fill in the gaps to find angle *p*.

AE = EF = FB = ... cm

Angle *q* = ...°

Angle *p* = ...°

. . . .

. . . .

2 marks

18 (a) A watering can holds 4.5 litres.
Each tomato plant needs 120 ml of water.
How many tomato plants can I water from a full watering can?

. . . . plants

. . . .

. . . .

2 marks

(b) A crop of tomatoes has a mass of 6.5 kg.
45% of their mass is water.
What is the mass of the water in the tomatoes?

. . . . kg

. . . .

1 mark

THIS IS THE END OF THE TIER 3–5 PAPER

THIS IS THE START OF THE TIER 6–8 PAPER

19 In my greenhouse are two plants.
Plant A is 20 cm tall and grows at 2 cm per day.
Plant B is 15 cm tall and grows at 3 cm per day.
Today the ratio of the heights of the plant A to plant B is 20 : 15, which can be simplified to 4 : 3.

(a) What will be the ratio of the height of plant A to the height of plant B tomorrow?
Write your answer as simply as possible.

. . . . : . . . .

....
1 mark

(b) After five days plant A is 30 cm tall. What will be the ratio of the height of plant A to the height of plant B then?

. . . . : . . . .

....
1 mark

(c) Could the ratio of the height of plant A to plant B ever have been 1.5 : 1?
Tick (✔) Yes or No

☐ Yes   ☐ No

Explain your answer.

. . . . : . . . .

....
1 mark

20 The squared paper shows the nets of a squared-based pyramid and a triangular prism.

(a)   Work out the surface area of each solid.

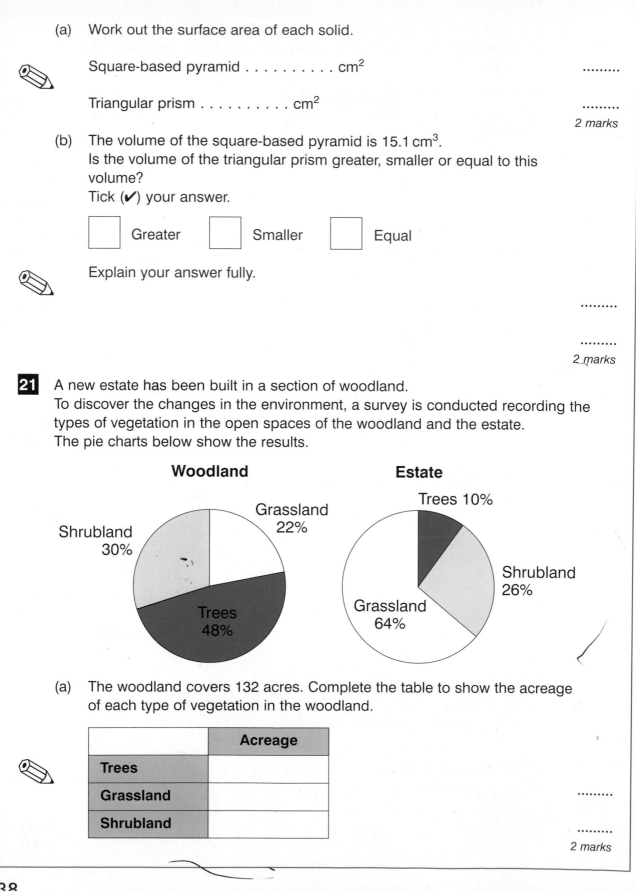

       Square-based pyramid . . . . cm²   . . . .

       Triangular prism . . . . cm²   . . . .

                                                                        2 marks

(b)   The volume of the square-based pyramid is 15.1 cm³.
       Is the volume of the triangular prism greater, smaller or equal to this
       volume?
       Tick (✔) your answer.

       ☐ Greater   ☐ Smaller   ☐ Equal

       Explain your answer fully.

                                                                        . . . .

                                                                        . . . .
                                                                        2 marks

21 A new estate has been built in a section of woodland.
        To discover the changes in the environment, a survey is conducted recording the
        types of vegetation in the open spaces of the woodland and the estate.
        The pie charts below show the results.

Woodland   **Estate**

Grassland 22%   Trees 10%
Shrubland 30%   Shrubland 26%
Trees 48%   Grassland 64%

(a)   The woodland covers 132 acres. Complete the table to show the acreage
       of each type of vegetation in the woodland.

	Acreage
Trees	
Grassland	
Shrubland	

                                                                        . . . .

                                                                        . . . .
                                                                        2 marks

(b) In the estate there are a total of 0.52 acres of trees.
Complete the table to show the acreage of each type of vegetation in
the estate.

	Acreage
Trees	0.52
Grassland	
Shrubland	

....

....

2 marks

(c) Building the estate has altered the proportions of each type of vegetation.
Write a sentence to describe these changes.

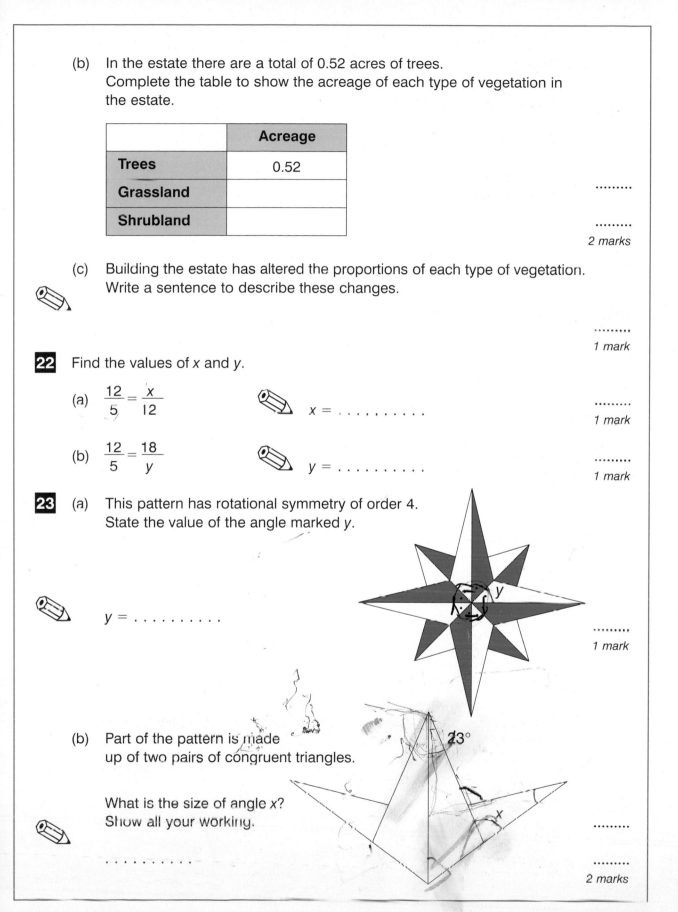

....

1 mark

22 Find the values of x and y.

(a) $\dfrac{12}{5} = \dfrac{x}{12}$ $x = \ldots\ldots\ldots\ldots$ ....   *1 mark*

(b) $\dfrac{12}{5} = \dfrac{18}{y}$ $y = \ldots\ldots\ldots\ldots$ ....   *1 mark*

23 (a) This pattern has rotational symmetry of order 4.
State the value of the angle marked y.

$y = \ldots\ldots\ldots\ldots$

....

1 mark

(b) Part of the pattern is made
up of two pairs of congruent triangles.

23°

What is the size of angle x?
Show all your working.

x

....

....

. . . .

2 marks

24 The information in the box describes three different circles A, B and C.

> The area of circle A is 20 cm².
> The radius of circle B is 20 cm.
> The circumference of circle C is 20 cm.

Put circles A, B and C in order of size, starting with the smallest.
Show all your working to explain your answer.

....

. . . .

   smallest   largest

....

2 marks

THIS IS THE END OF THE TIER 4–6 PAPER

25 On the square grid is shown a square with an area of S square units and an octagon with an area of T square units.

Squares and octagons can be put together to cover the grid. The shape shown on the right has an area of $S + 2T$ square units.

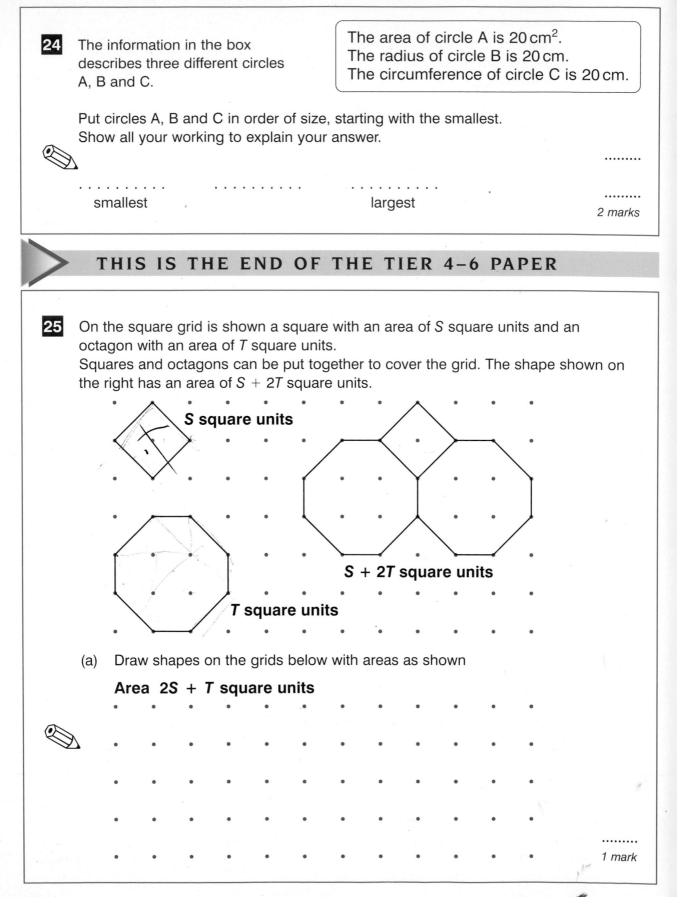

S square units

S + 2T square units

T square units

(a) Draw shapes on the grids below with areas as shown

Area 2S + T square units

....

1 mark

Area 2(S + T) square units

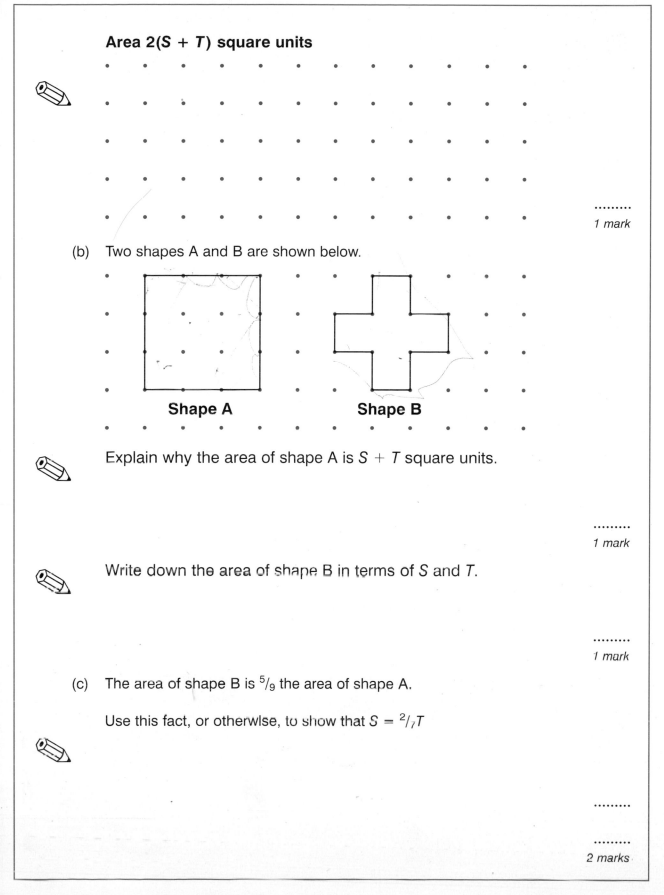

....
1 mark

(b) Two shapes A and B are shown below.

Shape A   **Shape B**

Explain why the area of shape A is $S + T$ square units.

....
1 mark

Write down the area of shape B in terms of S and T.

....
1 mark

(c) The area of shape B is $^5/_9$ the area of shape A.

Use this fact, or otherwise, to show that $S = ^2/_7 T$

....

....
2 marks

26 Sunflowers are one of the fastest growing plants.
A seedling is 3.5 cm tall.
Every day the plant grows by 6.5 cm.

(a) How long will the plant take to reach a height
of over 1 m?

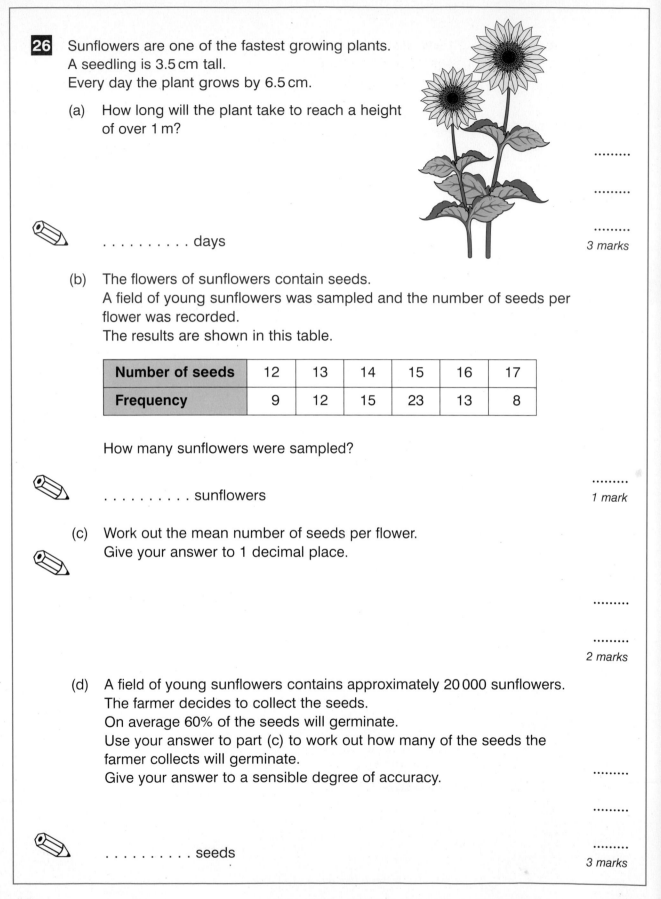

. . . . days

....

....

....
3 marks

(b) The flowers of sunflowers contain seeds.
A field of young sunflowers was sampled and the number of seeds per
flower was recorded.
The results are shown in this table.

Number of seeds	12	13	14	15	16	17
Frequency	9	12	15	23	13	8

How many sunflowers were sampled?

. . . . sunflowers

....
1 mark

(c) Work out the mean number of seeds per flower.
Give your answer to 1 decimal place.

....

....
2 marks

(d) A field of young sunflowers contains approximately 20 000 sunflowers.
The farmer decides to collect the seeds.
On average 60% of the seeds will germinate.
Use your answer to part (c) to work out how many of the seeds the
farmer collects will germinate.
Give your answer to a sensible degree of accuracy.

....

....

. . . . seeds

....
3 marks

27 Here are three pictures **which are drawn to scale**.
Picture B is a one-way stretch of picture A.
Picture C is an enlargement of picture A.

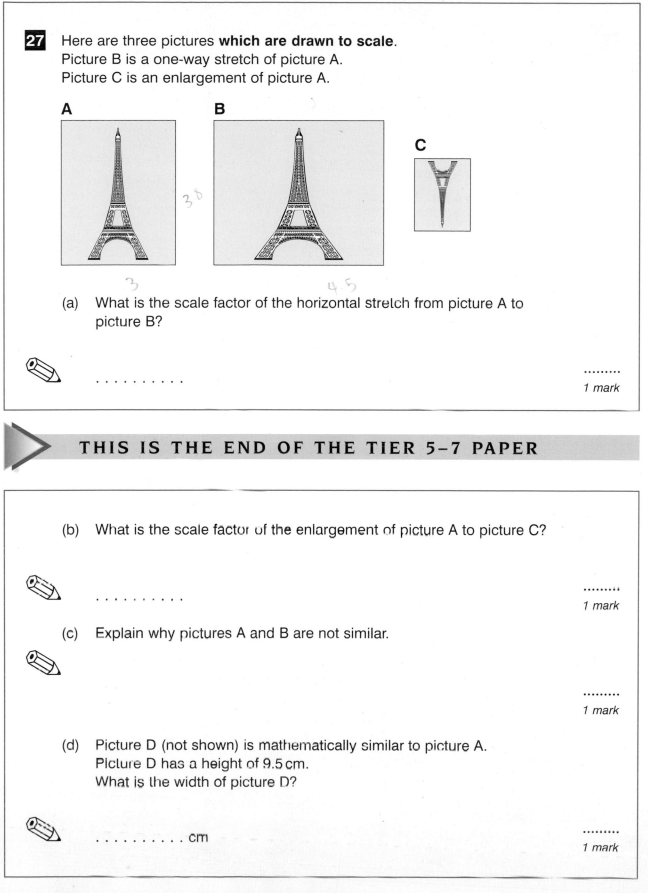

A   B

C

30

3   4.5

(a) What is the scale factor of the horizontal stretch from picture A to
picture B?

. . . .
                                                         1 mark

> ## THIS IS THE END OF THE TIER 5–7 PAPER

(b) What is the scale factor of the enlargement of picture A to picture C?

. . . .
                                                         1 mark

(c) Explain why pictures A and B are not similar.

                                                         . . . .
                                                         1 mark

(d) Picture D (not shown) is mathematically similar to picture A.
Picture D has a height of 9.5 cm.
What is the width of picture D?

. . . . cm   . . . .
                                                         1 mark

28 The diagram shows what percentage of the cost of a banana different people involved in the growing, shipping and sale of the banana receive.

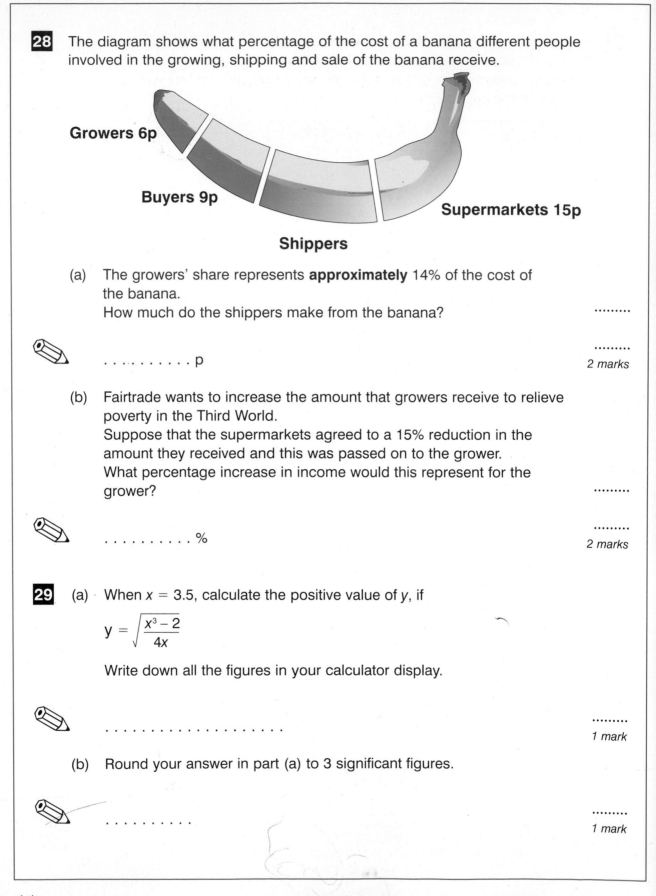

Growers 6p

Buyers 9p

Supermarkets 15p

Shippers

(a) The growers' share represents **approximately** 14% of the cost of the banana.
How much do the shippers make from the banana?

....

. . . . p

....
2 marks

(b) Fairtrade wants to increase the amount that growers receive to relieve poverty in the Third World.
Suppose that the supermarkets agreed to a 15% reduction in the amount they received and this was passed on to the grower.
What percentage increase in income would this represent for the grower?

....

. . . . %

....
2 marks

29 (a) When $x = 3.5$, calculate the positive value of y, if

$$y = \sqrt{\frac{x^3 - 2}{4x}}$$

Write down all the figures in your calculator display.

. . . .

....
1 mark

(b) Round your answer in part (a) to 3 significant figures.

. . . .

....
1 mark

30 The standard of living in countries is often measured by calculating how much each person spends on goods and services in a year.
This table shows this figure for the eight richest countries in the world, along with the population.

Country	Amount spent per person each year (US dollars)	Population
Switzerland	25 540	7.5×10^6
Japan	21 790	1.3×10^8
United States	19 720	2.8×10^8
Germany	16 610	8.1×10^7
France	16 080	5.9×10^7
Australia	13 390	1.9×10^7
United Kingdom	12 590	5.9×10^7
Canada	12 130	3.0×10^7

(a) Which country in the table has the largest population?

. . . .

. . . .
1 mark

(b) The *Total private consumption expenditure* for a country is calculated by multiplying the amount spent per person by the population.
Calculate the *Total private consumption expenditure* for the United Kingdom.
Give your answer in standard form.

. . . .

. . . .

. . . .
2 marks

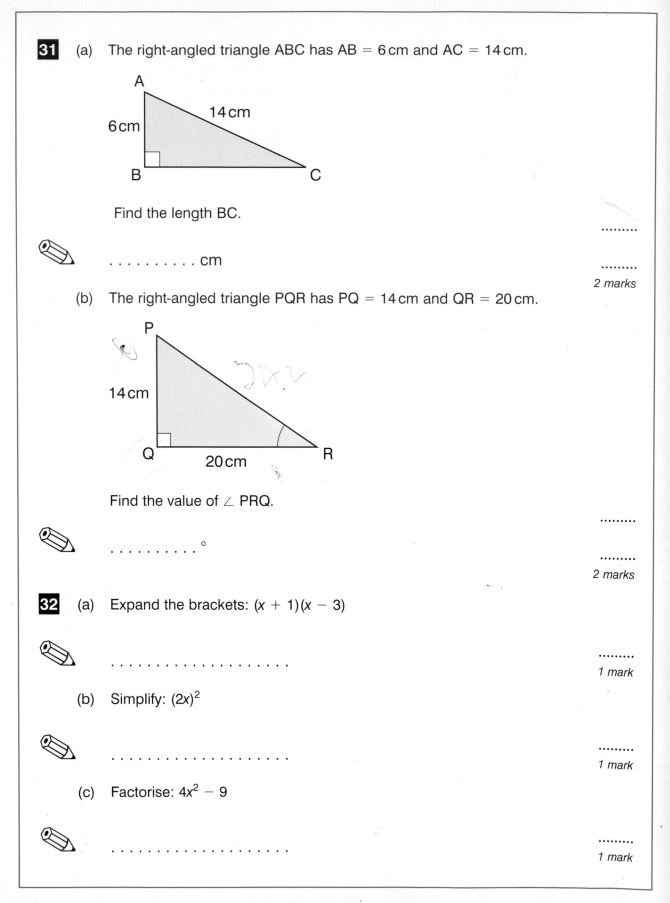

31   (a)   The right-angled triangle ABC has AB = 6 cm and AC = 14 cm.

A

14 cm

6 cm

B   C

Find the length BC.

. . . .

. . . . cm

. . . .

2 marks

(b)   The right-angled triangle PQR has PQ = 14 cm and QR = 20 cm.

P

14 cm

Q   20 cm   R

Find the value of ∠ PRQ.

. . . .

. . . . °

. . . .

2 marks

32   (a)   Expand the brackets: $(x + 1)(x - 3)$

. . . .

. . . .

1 mark

(b)   Simplify: $(2x)^2$

. . . .

. . . .

1 mark

(c)   Factorise: $4x^2 - 9$

. . . .

. . . .

1 mark

33 A cylinder has a volume of 225π cm^3.
The height is 16 cm.

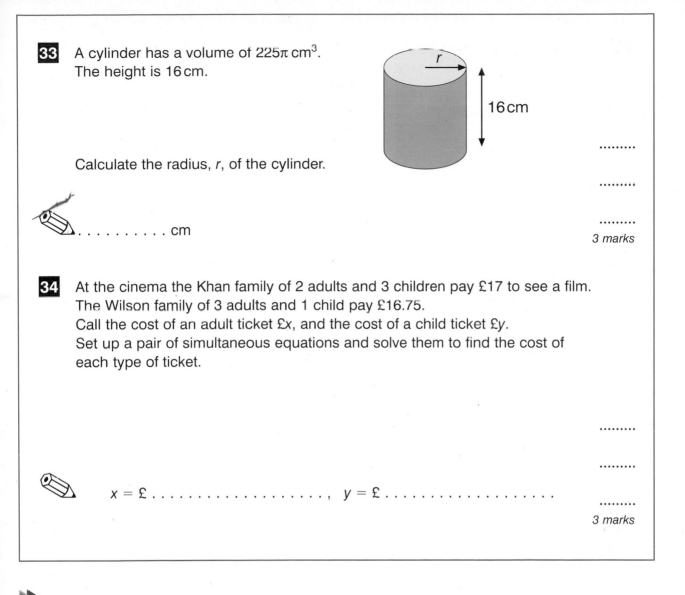

16 cm

Calculate the radius, r, of the cylinder.

.... cm

....

....

....

3 marks

34 At the cinema the Khan family of 2 adults and 3 children pay £17 to see a film.
The Wilson family of 3 adults and 1 child pay £16.75.
Call the cost of an adult ticket £x, and the cost of a child ticket £y.
Set up a pair of simultaneous equations and solve them to find the cost of
each type of ticket.

$x = £ \ldots\ldots\ldots\ldots\ldots\ldots , \quad y = £ \ldots\ldots\ldots\ldots\ldots$

....

....

....

3 marks

THIS IS THE END OF THE TIER 6–8 PAPER

Mental arithmetic test C (Tiers 3–5)

"For this first group of questions you will have 5 seconds to work out each answer and write it down."

	The Questions:
1	Write in figures the number two hundred and seven.
2	Divide thirty by six.
3	Your answer sheet shows the cost of a computer. What is this to the nearest hundred pounds?
4	Look at the equation. When q is 10 what is the value of p?
5	What is twenty-five per cent of forty pounds?
6	Multiply eight by nine.
7	Write a number that is bigger than a half but smaller than one.
8	Add two to minus seven.
9	I am thinking of a number. Call it x. I take three away from my number. Write an expression to show the result.

"For the next group of questions you will have 10 seconds to work out each answer and write it down."

	The Questions:
10	A late night film lasts for two and a half hours. It finishes at one thirty am. What time did it start? Answer in the twenty-four hour clock.
11	I am counting on in nought point threes. Four point three, four point six, four point nine, …. Write down the next two numbers.
12	Subtract twenty-two pence from seven pounds.
13	Shade one third of the diagram.
14	Add sixty-three and fifty-seven.
15	Two different lines are perpendicular. What is the angle between them?
16	One hundred families were asked where they went for their holidays. The bar chart shows the results. About how many families went to Spain?
17	Metres are a measure of length. Complete the sentence: Litres are a measure of ….

	The Questions:
18	How much is a third of six pounds thirty?
19	The diagram shows part of a map. The scale of the map is one centimetre to two and a half kilometres. The line between A and B is about 4 cm long. How far is the actual distance from A to B?
20	The pie chart shows the favourite National Tests subject of some pupils. Fifty pupils like English. How many like Maths?
21	Light travels at about three hundred thousand kilometres a second. Write this number in figures.
22	A worm is six inches long. About how many centimetres is that? Ring the best answer on the answer sheet.
23	Write a multiple of four between ninety and ninety-nine.
24	Look at at the angle. Estimate its size in degrees.
25	Look at the expression on the answer sheet. Write it as simply as possible.

"For the next group of questions you will have 15 seconds to work out each answer and write it down."

	The Questions:
26	Your answer sheet shows part of a train timetable. The train takes the same time between stations. Fill in the missing times.
27	Add together the numbers on your answer sheet.
28	Look at the grid. Complete the net so that it is a net of a cuboid.
29	A bag contains some red and black marbles. There are eight black marbles in the bag. The probability of taking a red marble from the bag is $\frac{1}{5}$. How many red marbles are there in the bag?
30	Your answer sheet shows the answer to the multiplication twenty-four by fifty-two. Use this information, or otherwise, to work out the answer to twelve multiplied by twenty-six.

Mental arithmetic test A/B (Tiers 4-6, 5-7, 6-8)

"For this first group of questions you will have 5 seconds to work out each answer and write it down."

	The Questions:
1	Multiply fifty-four by one hundred.
2	How many metres are there in one kilometre?
3	What is one-third of forty-eight?
4	Subtract four from minus six.
5	Look at the equation. When *y* is forty-nine, what is the value of *x*?
6	What is seven point five divided by two?
7	To the nearest kilogram the mass of a printer is nine kilograms. What is the least value the mass of the printer could be?

"For the next group of questions you will have 10 seconds to work out each answer and write it down."

	The Questions:
8	The chart shows the maximum temperatures in a resort during one year. How many months had a maximum temperature over twenty degrees?
9	A boat travels north for ten kilometres, then south-east for seven kilometres, then south-west for seven kilometres to return to where it started. What is the name of the shape of the boat's path?
10	On the grid, mark the point three-two with a cross.
11	Divide two by nought point one.
12	How far in kilometres is the distance ten miles? Circle the best answer on the answer sheet.
13	Look at the ratio. Write it in the form 1 : *n*.
14	The pie chart shows the favourite National Tests subject of some pupils. Fifty pupils like English. How many like Maths?
15	Two different lines are perpendicular. What is the angle between them?

	The Questions:
16	Look at the equation. Solve it to find the value of *x*.
17	A tomato plant is fifty centimetres tall. In a week it grows by ten per cent. How tall is it after a week?
18	What is the volume of a cuboid that is two metres long, one metre wide and fifty centimetres high?
19	What is a quarter of two thirds of sixty?
20	Look at the inequality. Write down all the solutions that are integers.

"For the next group of questions you will have 15 seconds to work out each answer and write it down."

	The Questions:
21	Write a factor of twenty-four that is an odd number other than one.
22	The first five odd numbers are one, three, five, seven and nine. What is the fiftieth odd number?
23	On the grid, sketch the line *x* plus *y* equals 5.
24	What is the approximate circumference of a circle with a radius of ten centimetres?
25	I have three cards with the digits one, five and six on them. I can make six different three-digit numbers with them. What is the difference between the largest and smallest numbers I can make?
26	Look at the calculation. Write down an approximate answer.
27	Complete the factorisation.
28	How many edges has a tetrahedron?
29	A bag contains some coloured marbles. The number of black and white marbles in the bag is shown. The probability of taking a red marble from the bag is $\frac{1}{5}$. How many red marbles are there in the bag?
30	I write down all the integers from one hundred to two hundred inclusive. How many zeros did I write down?

Paper 1

THIS IS THE START OF THE TIER 3–5 PAPER

Question 1

Part	Mark	Answer	Comments	Where to find more help
(a)	1	3 squares in 'No' row	• A ■ represents 4 pupils, so if 12 pupils say 'No', you need to show 3 squares because $12 \div 4 = 3$. • Your squares do not need to be drawn accurately.	*Level 3 Handling data*
(b)	1	9	• There are $4^{1}/_{2}$ circles to show how many pupils walk to school. As a circle represents 2 pupils, 9 pupils walk to school.	
Total	**2**			

Question 2

Part	Mark	Answer	Comments	Where to find more help
	1	Three numbers that add up to 12	• For example: $5 + 4 + 3$ or $9 + 2 + 1$ • The order of the numbers does not matter. • You can even use the same numbers: $4 + 4 + 4$ or $6 + 3 + 3$ • Negative numbers or zeros can also be used: $24 + (^-12) + 0$	*Level 4 Number* *This question is testing skills in the four operations on number.* See *Collins Revision Guide KS3 Maths*, page 1
	1	Two numbers multiplied to give 12	• For example: 2×6 or 3×4 or 1×12 • The order of the numbers does not matter.	
	1	Two numbers divided to give 12	• For example: $12 \div 1$ or $24 \div 2$ or $36 \div 3$ • You must make sure the two numbers are the correct way round for division. $1 \div 12$ would be marked wrong.	
Total	**3**			

Question 3

Part	Mark	Answer	Comments	Where to find more help
(a)	1	35	• There are ten divisions on the scale so one division represents 5. Starting from 25, the arrow is pointing to $25 + 5 + 5 = 35$.	*Level 4 Shape, space and measures* *This question is testing skills in reading and using scales.* See *Collins Revision Guide KS3 Maths*, page 28
(b)	1	50 — 40 — 30 ← 20 — 10 — 0 —	• Each division represents 10 so your arrow should be placed half-way between 30 and 40. • Your arrow does not need to be accurately positioned, provided your intention is clear.	
Total	**2**			

Question 4

Part	Mark	Answer	Comments	Where to find more help
(a)	1	45p	• You must have the p sign in the answer. • £0.45 would also be accepted. • Units are important when writing down money answers.	*Level 5 Number* *This question is testing skills in solving money problems.*
	1	60p	• £0.60 would also be accepted, but £0.6 would be marked wrong. • If you left out the money units for both answers, you would gain 1 mark out of 2.	
	1	£1.05	• The £ sign is given on the answer line, so your answer must be given in pounds. • £1.5 is wrong as this means £1.50. • Money answers in pounds should always have two decimal places.	
(b)	1	Any of the following correct ways: • two Fruit Gums • one Fruit Gums and two Refresher Bars • one Dolly Mixture and one Refresher Bar • one Jelly Babies and one Fizz Chew • two Fizz Chews and one Refresher Bar	• You could use abbreviations, provided your answers are clear. For example: 2 FG for two Fruit Gums	
	1	A different correct way from above.		
	1	Another different correct way from above.		
Total	6			

Question 5

Part	Mark	Answer	Comments	Where to find more help
(a)	1	Clock showing 5 o'clock	• On a 24-hour clock, remember to subtract 12 to get a pm time.	*Level 4 Number* *This question is testing skills in using the 24-hour clock.*
(b)	1	08:20	• Half an hour is 30 minutes, so ten to eight add on 30 minutes is twenty past eight.	
(c)	1	19:45	• A quarter to eight in the morning is 7:45, so in the evening a quarter to eight is 19:45. Remember to add 12 on to the hours on a 24-hour clock.	
Total	3			

Question 6

Part	Mark	Answer	Comments	Where to find more help
(a)	1	23	• This can be done by a subtraction. You should set it up like this: $\begin{array}{r} {}^5\!6\ {}^1 0 \\ -\ 3\ 7 \\ \hline 2\ 3 \end{array}$ • Another way to do the problem is to count on: 30 40 50 60 +3 +10 +10 = 23	*Level 4 Number* *This question is testing skills in using the four operations on number.* See *Collins Revision Guide KS3 Maths,* page 1
(b)	1	27	• This is another subtraction. You should set it up like this: $\begin{array}{r} {}^5\!6\ {}^1 0 \\ -\ 3\ 3 \\ \hline 2\ 7 \end{array}$	
(c)	1	110	• The addition should be set up like this: $\begin{array}{r} 3\ 7 \\ +\ 7\ 3 \\ \hline 1\ 1\ 0 \\ {}_{1\ 1} \end{array}$	
(d)	1	259	• The multiplication should be set up like this: $\begin{array}{r} 3\ 7 \\ \times\ \ 7 \\ \hline 2\ 5\ 9 \\ {}_4 \end{array}$ • Another way to do this problem is to work out $7 \times 30 = 210$ and $7 \times 7 = 49$, then add the answers: $210 + 49 = 259$	
Total	**4**			

THIS IS THE START OF THE TIER 4–6 PAPER

Question 7

Part	Mark	Answer	Comments	Where to find more help
(a)	1	4510	• The addition should be set up like this: $\begin{array}{r} 3\ 7\ 7\ 3 \\ +\ \ 7\ 3\ 7 \\ \hline 4\ 5\ 1\ 0 \\ {}_{1\ 1\ 1} \end{array}$	*Level 4 Number* *This question is testing skills in using the four operations on number.* See *Collins Revision Guide KS3 Maths,* page 1
(b)	1	3036	• The subtraction should set it up like this: $\begin{array}{r} 3\ 7\ {}^6\!7\ {}^1 3 \\ -\ \ \ 7\ 3\ 7 \\ \hline 3\ 0\ 3\ 6 \end{array}$	
Total	**2**			

Question 8

Part	Mark	Answer	Comments	Where to find more help
(a)	1	240 and 480	• For doubling, you could either work out 120×2 or $120 + 120 = 240$ and then do the same again: 240×2 or $240 + 240 = 480$	*Level 4 Algebra* **This question is testing skills in recognising number patterns.** See *Collins Revision Guide KS3 Maths,* page 13
(b)	1	12.5 and 25	• The number chain in reverse is halving or dividing by 2: $50 \div 2 = 25$ and $25 \div 2 = 12.5$ or $12\frac{1}{2}$	
Total	2			

Question 9

Part	Mark	Answer	Comments	Where to find more help
	2	4, 8, 12, 16, 20	• 'Certain' here means that all the numbers must be multiples of 4: these are numbers in your 4 times table: 4, 8, 12, 16, 20, 24, 28, … • For it to be impossible that the numbers are greater than 20 means that all the numbers must be less than 21. • Only 4, 8, 12, 16 and 20 satisfy both conditions. The numbers can be given in any order. • If you gave any five multiples of 4 or any five numbers less than 20, you would gain 1 mark.	*Level 4 Algebra* **This question is testing understanding of multiples.** See *Collins Revision Guide KS3 Maths,* page 16
Total	2			

Question 10

Part	Mark	Answer	Comments	Where to find more help
	1	8	• Town A is an example to show you how to find the increase. It is the difference between 3 and 12. So work out: $12 - 3 = 9$ • For Town B, the difference between $^-3$ and 5 is: $5 - (^-3) = 5 + 3 = 8$ • Another way to answer the problem is to draw a number line to find the difference between $^-3$ and 5:	*Level 5 Number* **This question is testing skills in using negative numbers.** See *Collins Revision Guide KS3 Maths,* page 51
			+8 $^-3$ $^-2$ $^-1$ 0 1 2 3 4 5	
	1	1	• If the increase is 5, for Town C, you need to work out: $^-6 + 5$. So $^-6 + 5 = ^-1$ • Another way to answer the problem is to draw a number line and add 5 to $^-6$:	
			+5 $^-6$ $^-5$ $^-4$ $^-3$ $^-2$ $^-1$ 0	

Part	Mark	Answer	Comments	Where to find more help
	1	⁻8	• If the increase is 20, for Town D, you need to work out: 12 − 20. So 12 − 20 = ⁻8 • Another way to answer the problem is to draw a number line and subtract 20 from 12: −20 ⁻8 ⁻6 ⁻4 ⁻2 0 2 4 6 8 10 12	
Total	3			

Question 11

Part	Mark	Answer	Comments	Where to find more help
(a)	2	[graph: Spinner B vs Spinner A, points at (2,5), (3,4), (4,3)]	• Only three points have a total of 7: (4, 3), (3, 4) and (2, 5) • You would gain 1 mark if you plotted two points correctly.	*Level 4 Algebra* *This question is testing skills in using coordinates.* See *Collins Revision Guide KS3 Maths,* page 19
(b)	2	[graph: Spinner B vs Spinner A, points at (1,1), (2,2), (3,3), (4,4)]	• Four points have the same number: (1, 1), (2, 2), (3, 3) and (4, 4) • You would gain 1 mark if you plotted two or three points correctly.	
(c)	1	2 more than on Spinner A	• Write down the coordinates to spot the pattern: (0, 2), (1, 3), (2, 4) and (3, 5)	
Total	5			

Question 12

Part	Mark	Answer	Comments	Where to find more help
(a)	1	Tick 'Yes' box **and** Both shapes have an area of 6 squares.	• Area is the amount of space inside a 2-D shape Both shapes have an area of 6 squares, so their areas are the same.	*Level 4 Shape, space and measures* *This question is testing understanding of perimeter and area.* See *Collins Revision Guide KS3 Maths,* page 29
(b)	1	Tick 'No' box **and** Perimeter of shapes are 10 and 12.	• Perimeter is the total distance around a 2-D shape. The perimeter of the rectangle is 10 units and the perimeter of the other shape is 12 units, so their perimeters are not the same.	
Total	**2**			

Question 13

Part	Mark	Answer	Comments	Where to find more help
	2	1.5 litres	• The capacity of the two large bottles $= 3.7 - 0.7 = 3$ litres. So the capacity of one large bottle $= 3 \div 2 = 1.5$ litres or $1\frac{1}{2}$ litres. • You would gain 1 mark if you showed the correct method: $\frac{3.7 - 0.7}{2}$ but made an error in the calculation.	*Level 4 Number* *This question is testing skills in adding and subtracting decimals.* See *Collins Revision Guide KS3 Maths,* page 6
Total	**2**			

Question 14

Part	Mark	Answer	Comments	Where to find more help
(a)	1		• You can use tracing paper to help you. • You could show the line of symmetry on the diagram if you wish.	*Level 4 Shape, space and measures* *This question is testing understanding of symmetry.* See *Collins Revision Guide KS3 Maths,* page 26
(b)	1		• Again use tracing paper to help you. • You could show the lines of symmetry on the diagram if you wish.	

Part	Mark	Answer	Comments	Where to find more help
(c)	1		• Again use tracing paper to help you. • The order of rotational symmetry is the number of times the shape will fit on top of itself during one rotation. There are four ways of doing this: 	
Total	**3**			

Question 15

Part	Mark	Answer	Comments	Where to find more help
(a)	1	$6a + 5b$	• This question is about collecting like terms. • First collect the as together: $2a + 4a = 6a$, then collect the bs together: $3b + 2b = 5b$ • $5b + 6a$ is the same answer. • Remember that a and b are different variables, and so cannot be added together. An answer of $11ab$ would gain no marks. • You would not gain any marks if you wrote for example: $6a$ as $6 \times a$ or $a6$	*Level 5 Algebra* *This question is testing manipulation of simple formulae.* See *Collins Revision Guide KS3 Maths*, page 63
(b)	1	$3x + 7$	• First collect the xs together: $5x - 2x = 3x$ Then collect the numbers together: $8 - 1 = 7$ • $7 + 3x$ is the same answer. • Remember that the variable x cannot be added to a number. An answer of $10x$ would gain no marks.	
Total	**2**			

THIS IS THE START OF THE TIER 5–7 PAPER

Question 16

Part	Mark	Answer	Comments	Where to find more help
	2	6 0 0 4 1 0 2 2 0 2 0 1 0 3 0 0 1 1	• There are five rows left blank in the table, so this is a clue that you are looking for five different combinations. • Always check that you have not repeated a combination. • If you wrote down four correct combinations, you would gain 1 mark.	*Level 4 Algebra* *This question is testing understanding of number patterns.* See *Collins Revision Guide KS3 Maths*, page 13
Total	**2**			

Question 17

Part	Mark	Answer	Comments	Where to find more help
(a)	1	60	• All you need to do is double 30.	*Level 5 Number* **This question is testing understanding of fractional parts.** See *Collins Revision Guide KS3 Maths,* page 52
(b)	1	40	• If $^3/_4$ of a number is 30, then $^1/_4$ is $30 \div 3 = 10$. So the number must be $10 \times 4 = 40$. • A diagram may help you. $^3/_4$ of the shape is shaded. 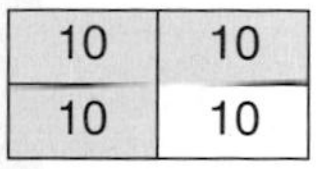 <table><tr><td>10</td><td>10</td></tr><tr><td>10</td><td>10</td></tr></table>	
(c)	1	45	• If $^2/_3$ of a number is 30, then $^1/_3$ is $30 \div 2 = 15$. So the number must be $15 \times 3 = 45$. A diagram may help you. $^2/_3$ of the shape is shaded.  <table><tr><td>15</td><td>15</td><td>15</td></tr></table>	
Total	**3**			

Question 18

Part	Mark	Answer	Comments	Where to find more help
(a)	1	(⁻1, 3)	• The diagram shows the triangle ABC moved three squares to the left. 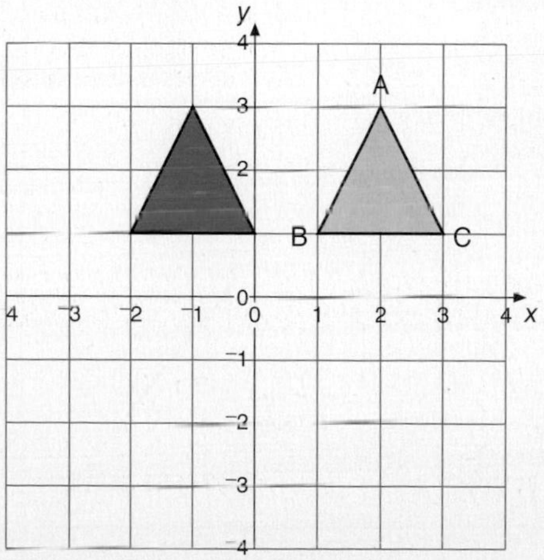 • When giving coordinates, remember that the x-coordinate is written first.	*Level 5 Algebra* **This question is testing understanding of coordinates in all four quadrants.** See *Collins Revision Guide KS3 Maths,* page 64
(b)	1	(⁻3, ⁻2)	• Since the triangle moves off the grid, you will need to start at the point C, count six squares to the left and three squares down. • When giving coordinates, remember that the x-coordinate is written first.	
Total	**2**			

Question 19

Part	Mark	Answer	Comments	Where to find more help
(a)	1	6	• The median is found by listing the numbers in order (which they already are) and then finding the exact middle value. ~~2~~ 4 8 ~~12~~ ↑ There are two values in the middle, so the median is the value exactly between these two. Hence the median is 6. • Another way to find the value exactly between 4 and 8 is to work out $\frac{4+8}{2}$.	*Level 4 Handling data* *This question is about the median.* See *Collins Revision Guide KS3 Maths,* page 38
(b)	1	3, 8 and 9	• If the median age is 8, then the three ages in order have the value 8 in the middle: ___ 8 ___ • Since the three ages add up to 20, the other two ages add up to 12. • If the range of the three ages is 6, then you need to find two numbers, which add up to 12 and have a difference of 6. The two numbers are 3 and 9.	*Level 5 Handling data* *This question is about the range.* See *Collins Revision Guide KS3 Maths,* page 84
Total	**2**			

Question 20

Part	Mark	Answer	Comments	Where to find more help
	2	Triangle drawn correctly: 5 cm 60° 6 cm	• 1 mark is given for drawing the angle of 60°, within a tolerance of 2°, and 1 mark for completing the triangle correctly.	*Level 5 Shape, space and measures* *This question tests skills in drawing accurately.*
Total	**2**			

Question 21

Part	Mark	Answer	Comments	Where to find more help
(a)	2	£487.50	• This is long multiplication. • It is easier to work in pence when doing the multiplication. $$\begin{array}{r} 1\,2\,5\,0 \\ \times\quad 3\,9 \\ \hline 3\,7\,5\,0\,0 \\ 1\,1\,2\,5\,0 \\ \hline 4\,8\,7\,5\,0 \end{array}$$ 48750p = £487.50 • You can also do the long multiplication by the Napier's bones method. • Your answer must be in pounds and if you got one digit wrong in the answer, you would gain 1 mark.	*Level 5 Number* *This question is testing skills in long multiplication.* See *Collins Revision Guide KS3 Maths,* page 44
(b)	2	£14	• This is long division. • You will have probably set your working out as below. $$\begin{array}{r} 1\,4 \\ 39\,\overline{)\,5\,4\,6} \\ -3\,9 \\ \hline 1\,5\,6 \\ -1\,5\,6 \\ \hline 0\,0\,0 \end{array}$$ • Another way to do this problem is to use the method of repeated subtraction: $$\begin{array}{r} 5\,4\,6 \\ 10 \times 39 = 3\,9\,0 \\ \hline 1\,5\,6 \\ 4 \times 39 = 1\,5\,6 \\ \hline 0\,0\,0 \end{array}$$ $10 + 4 = 14$ • If you made one error in the calculation, you would gain just 1 mark.	*Level 5 Number* *This question is testing skills in long division.* See *Collins Revision Guide KS3 Maths,* page 46
Total	**4**			

Part	Mark	Answer	Comments	Where to find more help
(a)	1	$a = 5$	• $4a + 3 = 23$ (Subtract 3 from both sides) $\quad 4a = 20$ (Divide both sides by 4) $\quad\ \ a = 5$ • You can also solve this type of equation by using a flow chart method. $a \rightarrow \boxed{\times 4} \rightarrow \boxed{+3} \rightarrow 23$ $5 \leftarrow \boxed{\div 4} \leftarrow \boxed{-3} \leftarrow 23$	*Level 6 Algebra* *This question is testing skills in solving linear equations.* See *Collins Revision Guide KS3 Maths*, page 117
(b)	1	$b = 2\frac{1}{2}$ or 2.5	• $2b - 1 = 4$ (Add 1 to both sides) $\quad 2b = 5$ (Divide both sides by 2) $\quad\ \ b = 2\frac{1}{2}$ • You can also solve this type of equation by using a flow chart method. $b \rightarrow \boxed{\times 2} \rightarrow \boxed{-1} \rightarrow 4$ $2\frac{1}{2} \leftarrow \boxed{\div 2} \leftarrow \boxed{+1} \leftarrow 4$	
Total	**2**			

THIS IS THE END OF THE TIER 3–5 PAPER

THIS IS THE START OF THE TIER 6–8 PAPER

Question 23

Part	Mark	Answer	Comments	Where to find more help
(a)	2	$x = 3\frac{1}{2}$	• Rearrange the equation, so that all the xs are on one side and all the numbers are on the other side. • $5x - 6 = 3x + 1$ (Subtract $3x$ from both sides) $\quad 2x - 6 = 1$ (Add 6 to both sides) $\quad\quad 2x = 7$ (Divide both sides by 2) $\quad\quad\ \ x = 3.5$ or $3\frac{1}{2}$ • You would gain 1 mark if you did one of these steps correctly: $2x - 6 = 1$ or $5x = 3x + 7$	*Level 6 Algebra* *This question is testing skills in solving linear equations.* See *Collins Revision Guide KS3 Maths*, page 117
(b)	2	$y = {}^-2$	• $3(2y + 5) = 3$ (Expand the brackets) $\quad 6y + 15 = 3$ (Subtract 15 from both sides) $\quad\quad\ \ 6y = {}^-12$ (Divide both sides by 6) $\quad\quad\ \ \ y = {}^-2$ • You would gain 1 mark if you managed to get as far as $6y = {}^-12$.	
Total	**4**			

60

Question 24

Part	Mark	Answer	Comments	Where to find more help
	3	A = 75°, B = 100°, C = 105°	• The sum of the angles in a quadrilateral is 360°. • Now form an equation by summing the four angles: $x + 25° + 2x + 2x + 5° + 80 = 360°$ Simplifying the equation gives: $5x + 110° = 360°$ (Subtract 110° from both sides) $5x = 250°$ (Divide both sides by 5) $x = 50°$ • The three unknown angles can now be calculated: $\angle A = x + 25° = 75°$ $\angle B = 2x = 100°$ $\angle C = 2x + 5° = 105°$ • Remember to check that the four angles add up to 360°. • 1 mark is for obtaining the correct equation, 1 mark for solving the equation correctly and 1 mark for obtaining three correct angles.	*Level 6 Shape, space and measures* *This question is testing understanding of angle properties of polygons.* See *Collins Revision Guide KS3 Maths,* page 133
Total	**3**			

Question 25

Part	Mark	Answer	Comments	Where to find more help
(a)	1	$\frac{16}{10}$ or $1\frac{3}{5}$	• Since both fractions have the same denominator, the addition is straightforward: $\frac{7}{10} + \frac{9}{10} = \frac{16}{10}$ • The answer can be written as a top-heavy fraction or as a mixed number.	*Level 6 Number* *This question is testing skills in adding and subtracting fractions.* See *Collins Revision Guide KS3 Maths,* page 109
	1	Arrow at $1\frac{3}{5}$	• Each division on the number line is $\frac{1}{5}$. • If you gave the answer to part (a) as $\frac{16}{20}$ or $\frac{8}{10}$ and showed this correctly on the number line, you would gain 1 mark.	
(b)	1	27	• $2\frac{7}{10} = \frac{27}{10}$, so there are 27 tenths altogether. You would still gain 1 mark if you left your answer as $\frac{27}{10}$.	
(c)	2	3	• This is a division of fractions. Part (b) helps you realise that with a division, all fractions must be made top heavy first. • The easiest way to do this problem is to think in tenths. 27 tenths divided by 9 tenths is 3. • You can invert the second fraction, multiply and then cancel down: $\frac{27}{10} \div \frac{9}{10} = \frac{27^3}{10_1} \times \frac{10^1}{9_1} = \frac{3}{1} = 3$	
Total	**5**			

Question 26

Part	Mark	Answer	Comments	Where to find more help
(a)	1	$8x + 11y$	• The perimeter is found by adding together the three sides and then simplifying the expression: $5x + 6y + 3x + 5y = 8x + 11y$	*Level 6 Shape, space and measures* *This question is testing understanding of perimeter and area.*
	1	$15xy$	• The formula for the area of a triangle is $A = \frac{1}{2}bh$ where b is the base and h is the perpendicular height. The area of the triangle is therefore $A = \frac{1}{2} \times 6y \times 5x = \frac{1}{2} \times 30xy = 15xy$ • This is the same as $15yx$ but it is usual to keep the letters in alphabetical order.	See *Collins Revision Guide KS3 Maths,* page 139
(b)	1	$4x$	• Here you are given the area and need to find h. Using the formula for the area of a triangle gives the equation: $6x^2 = \frac{1}{2} \times 3x \times h$ (Multiply both sides by 2) $12x^2 = 3xh$ (Divide both sides by $3x$) $h = 4x$	
Total	**3**			

Question 27

Part	Mark	Answer	Comments	Where to find more help
(a)	1	234×15	• Try not to use trial and error methods for this part of the question: look for number patterns. This is 4 as 3510 ends in 0 and 2 is used. $3510 = \boxed{2}\;\boxed{}\;\boxed{} \times \boxed{}\;\boxed{5}$ This must be 1 or 3. It cannot be 3 as $200 \times 30 = 6000$ which is too big.	*Level 5 Number* *This question is testing skills in long multiplication and long division.*
	1	254×31	• This is 1. $7874 = \boxed{}\;\boxed{}\;\boxed{4} \times \boxed{3}\;\boxed{}$ This must be 2 or 5. It cannot be 5 as $500 \times 30 = 15000$ which is too big.	See *Collins Revision Guide KS3 Maths,* page 44
(b)	1	132	• This can be done by long division. $\begin{array}{r} 1\,3\,2 \\ 45\,\overline{)5\,9\,4\,0} \\ -4\,5 \\ \hline 1\,4\,4 \\ -1\,3\,5 \\ \hline 9\,0 \\ -9\,0 \\ \hline 0\,0 \end{array}$ • You may also notice that the units number must be a 2 otherwise there would be a remainder and the hundreds column must be a 1 as $100 \times 45 =$ which is close to 5940.	
Total	**3**			

Question 28

Part	Mark	Answer	Comments	Where to find more help
(a)	1	$y = 3$	• Lines that are drawn horizontally, parallel to the x-axis, are of the form $y = a$, where a is the value where the line crosses the y-axis. The equation of the line is therefore $y = 3$. You would gain no marks if you wrote 'y is 3'	*Level 6 Algebra* *This question is testing skill in drawing linear graphs.* See *Collins Revision Guide KS3 Maths,* page 123
	1	$x = {}^-4$	• Lines that are drawn vertically, parallel to the y-axis, are of the form $x = b$, where b is the value where the line crosses the x-axis. The equation of the line is therefore $x = {}^-4$. You would gain no marks if you wrote 'x is ${}^-4$'.	
Total	**2**			

> ## THIS IS THE END OF THE TIER 4–6 PAPER

Question 28 (continued)

Part	Mark	Answer	Comments	Where to find more help
(b)	1	AC → $y = {}^-{}^1/_2 x + 1$	• Lines that go diagonally across a graph are of the form $y = mx + c$, where m is the gradient of the line and c is the value where the line crosses the y-axis. • The diagonal AC has a gradient of ${}^-{}^1/_2$ and crosses the y-axis at 1, so $m = {}^-{}^1/_2$ and $c = 1$.	*Level 6 Algebra* *This question is testing understanding of gradient.* See *Collins Revision Guide KS3 Maths,* page 121
	1	BD → $y = {}^1/_2 x$	• The diagonal BD has a gradient of ${}^1/_2$ and crosses the y-axis at 0, so $m = {}^1/_2$ and $c = 0$.	
Total	**2**			

Question 29

Part	Mark	Answer	Comments	Where to find more help
(a)	1	12 points plotted on the scatter graph 	• Your points need to be plotted correctly.	*Level 6 Handling data* *This question is testing understanding of scatter diagrams.* See *Collins Revision Guide KS3 Maths,* page 148

Part	Mark	Answer	Comments	Where to find more help
(b)	1	Positive correlation	• You would gain one mark if you wrote 'the greater the height, the greater the mass'.	
(c)	1	Line of best fit drawn	• See part (a). Your line of best fit should pass between the points with about the same number of points on each side of the line.	*Level 7 Handling data* *This question is about lines of best fit.* See *Collins Revision Guide KS3 Maths,* page 204
(d)	1	It does not fit the correlation or it is an outlier.	• You could also write 'his point on the graph is too far away from the line of best fit' to gain 1 mark.	
Total	**4**			

Question 30

Part	Mark	Answer	Comments	Where to find more help
(a)	1	$\dfrac{14}{43}$	• There are 43 pupils in total and 14 of them are in Class 9KE. • In this question all probabilities should be written as fractions. A probability written as a ratio, 14 : 43, or in words, 14 out of 43, would not be acceptable.	*Level 6 Handling data* *This question is testing understanding of probability.* See *Collins Revision Guide KS3 Maths,* page 150
(b)	1	$\dfrac{8}{43}$	• There are 43 pupils in total and 8 of them are girls in Class 9HW.	
(c)	1	$\dfrac{9}{14}$	• There are 14 pupils in Class 9RH and 9 of them are boys.	
Total	**3**			

Question 31

Part	Mark	Answer	Comments	Where to find more help
(a)	1	65 mph	• In this question you need to know the formula for average speed is: $\text{Average speed} = \dfrac{\text{total distance travelled}}{\text{total time taken}}$ $= \dfrac{130}{2} = 65$ • The unit for speed is miles per hour or mph. If you missed the units out in this part of the question you would not gain the mark.	*Level 7 Shape, space and measures* *This question is about compound measures.* See *Collins Revision Guide KS3 Maths,* page 190
(b)	1	60 mph	• Average speed $= \dfrac{90}{1^{1/2}} = \dfrac{180}{3} = 60$ • Provided you gave the correct units in part (a), you would still gain 1 mark if you omitted the units in this part.	

Part	Mark	Answer	Comments	Where to find more help
(c)	2	55 mph	• You are finding an average speed for the **whole** journey. The total distance travelled is 220 miles and the total time taken is 2 hours + ½ hour + 1½ hours = 4 hours. So the average speed = $\frac{220}{4}$ = 55 • Remember to include the 30 minute (½ hour) stop at the service station. • If you write down the numbers 220 and 4 but get the wrong answer you would gain 1 mark.	
Total	4			

Question 32

Part	Mark	Answer	Comments	Where to find more help
(a)	1	$x = 75$	• This part involves substitution into formulae. $x = \dfrac{3 \times 5^3}{5} = \dfrac{3 \times \overset{25}{\cancel{125}}}{\underset{1}{\cancel{5}}} = \dfrac{75}{1} = 75$ • Notice how the cancelling down makes the calculation easier.	*Level 7 Number* *This question involves substitution in formulae.*
	1	$y = 2.9$ or $2\frac{9}{10}$	• $y = \dfrac{25 + 4}{10} = \dfrac{29}{10} = 2.9$ • The answer can be written as a decimal or a fraction.	
(b)	1	$2p - 3$	• This part involves expanding brackets. You need to know that $a(b + c) = ab + ac$ and $-a(b + c) = -ab - ac$. $3(2p + 1) - 2(3 + 2p)$ $= 6p + 3 - 6 - 4p = 2p - 3$ Notice the change in sign when expanding the second bracket.	*Level 7 Algebra* *This question involves expanding brackets.* See *Collins Revision Guide KS3 Maths,* page 178
	2	$4s^2 + 3s - 6$	• $s(s + 3) + 3(s^2 - 2)$ $= s^2 + 3s + 3s^2 - 6$ $= 4s^2 + 3s - 6$ Notice how the s^2 terms are collected together. • You would gain 1 mark if one of the three terms is incorrect.	
Total	5			

Question 33

Part	Mark	Answer	Comments	Where to find more help
	2	The completed diagram should look like this:	• This is a locus question. • First measure the line to find the scale. XY is 8 cm, so the scale used is 1 cm represents 20 km. • First draw a circle, centre at X, with a radius of 6 cm. Then draw a circle, centre at Y, with a radius of 5 cm. The region required is where the two circles intersect and should be shaded. • Some allowance is made for diagrams that are slightly inaccurate. You are expected to show that you can use a ruler and a pair of compasses. • You would gain 1 mark if one of your circles is drawn correctly.	*Level 7 Shape, space and measures* *This question is testing understanding of loci.* See *Collins Revision Guide KS3 Maths,* page 187
Total	**2**			

Question 34

Part	Mark	Answer	Comments	Where to find more help
(a)	1	$x - 1$ and $x + 1$ are both odd, so odd $\times$ odd = odd.	• The following need to be known for odd (O) and even (E) numbers: O $\times$ O = O, E $\times$ E = E and O $\times$ E = E $\times$ O = E • You would not gain the mark if you gave examples using particular numerical values for x.	*Level 7 Algebra* *This question involves odd and even numbers.*
(b)	2	y^2 is odd, $2y$ is even, so odd + even +1 = even	• $y^2 = y \times y$, so if y is odd, y^2 is also odd. You would gain 1 mark if you gave this explanation. • You would not gain any marks if you gave examples using particular numerical values for y.	
Total	**3**			

THIS IS THE END OF THE TIER 5–7 PAPER

Question 35

Part	Mark	Answer	Comments	Where to find more help
(a)	1	$(x - 3)(x + 2)$	• Factorise means write the expression as a product of two brackets in the form $(x + a)(x + b)$. To find the values of a and b, you need to find two numbers which have a product of $^-6$ and a sum of $^-1$. The two numbers are $^-3$ and $^+2$.	*Level 7 Algebra* *This question involves factorising and expanding brackets.* See *Collins Revision Guide KS3 Maths,* page 178
(b)	1	$x = 3$ or $x = ^-2$	• If $(x - 3)(x + 2) = 0$, then either bracket must also equal zero. So $(x - 3) = 0$ or $(x + 2) = 0$ Hence the two solutions are $x = 3$ or $x = ^-2$.	
Total	**2**			

Question 36

Part	Mark	Answer	Comments	Where to find more help
(a)	2	Show at least two points lie on the line. For example: any two of the points $(0, 8)$, $(1, 6)$, $(2, 4)$, $(3, 2)$, $(4, 0)$,	• You need to substitute two coordinate points into the equation of the line. For example, $(3, 2)$ lies on the line and $2 \times 3 + 2 = 8$, so $(3, 2)$ must lie on the line with equation $2x + y = 8$. • You would gain 1 mark for showing only one point lies on the line.	*Level 6 Algebra* *This question is testing understanding of linear graphs.* See *Collins Revision Guide KS3 Maths,* page 123
(b)	1	$^-2$	• First notice that the line has a negative gradient. $\dfrac{\text{The gradient}}{\text{of a line}} = \dfrac{\text{increase in } y}{\text{increase in } x}$ Using the triangle where the line crosses the axes: so the gradient is $\dfrac{^-8}{4} = ^-2$	
(c)	1	$y = ^-2x$	• Lines that go diagonally across a graph are of the form $y = mx + c$, where m is the gradient of the line and c is where the line crosses the x–axis. • The line parallel to the line $2x + y = 8$ has the same gradient of $^-2$, so $m = ^-2$ The line passes through the origin, so $c = 0$ The equation of the line is therefore $y = ^-2x$.	
Total	**4**			

Question 37

Part	Mark	Answer	Comments	Where to find more help
(a)	1	1, 4, 11, 23, 27, 30, 32	• Add each frequency to the sum of all the previous frequencies.	*Level 8 Handling data*
(b)	1	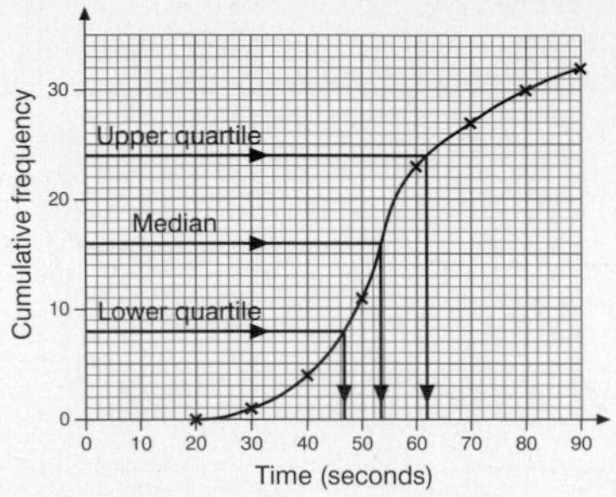	• The cumulative frequency graph is shown below. Notice that the points are plotted at the end of each interval.	*This question is testing understanding of cumulative frequency diagrams.* See *Collins Revision Guide KS3 Maths,* page 218
(c)	1	54 seconds	• The median is read from the middle of the cumulative frequency scale, at $32 \div 2 = 16$. The value is then read off the time scale as shown on the graph above. • An answer between 53 seconds and 55 seconds is acceptable.	
(d)	2	16 seconds	• The interquartile range is found by reading across from the quarter and three-quarter values of the cumulative frequency scale. These are 8 and 24. Reading the values off the time scale as shown on the graph above, the lower quartile is about 46 seconds and the upper quartile is about 62 seconds. The interquartile range is the difference between the two quartiles: $62 - 46 = 16$ seconds. • An answer between 15 seconds and 18 seconds is acceptable. • You would gain 1 mark for showing a correct method to find the quartiles, so it is important to show the arrows on the graph.	
(e)	1	The pensioners, because the median is higher or the range is smaller	• You could also say that the smaller range shows that the pensioners are more consistent.	
Total	**6**			

Question 38

Part	Mark	Answer	Comments	Where to find more help
(a)	2	$a < -6$	• Inequalities are solved in the same way as equations. $\dfrac{3 - 2a}{5} > 3$ (Multiply both sides by 5) $3 - 2a > 15$ (Add 2a to both sides) $3 > 2a + 15$ (Swap the inequality round) $2a + 15 < 3$ (Subtract 15 from both sides) $2a < ^-12$ (Divide both sides by 2) $a < ^-6$ • You would gain 1 mark if you solved the inequality as a equation and gave the answer as $a = ^-6$.	*Level 7 Algebra* *This question is testing skills in solving inequalities.* See *Collins Revision Guide KS3 Maths*, page 176
(b)	1	Any number with $b < ^-5$ is a solution.	• For example: $(^-6)^2 = 36$ Only one example is needed to gain the mark.	
Total	**3**			

Question 39

Part	Mark	Answer	Comments	Where to find more help
(a)	1	OX and OY are radii, so triangle OXY is an isosceles triangle.	• You must explain why the triangle is isosceles.	*Level 7 Shape, space and measures*
(b)	1	$\angle XOY - 180° - 2x$ (Angles in a triangle) $\angle XOZ = 180° - \angle XOY$ (Angles on a straight line) So $\angle XOZ = 180° - (180° - 2x) = 2x$	• You must explain each step in the proof. • You would not gain the mark if you took a numerical value for x.	
Total	**2**			

THIS IS THE END OF THE TIER 6–8 PAPER

Paper 2

THIS IS THE START OF THE TIER 3–5 PAPER

Question 1

Part	Mark	Answer	Comments	Where to find more help
(a)	1	C; Because it has 8 sides.	• An octagon has 8 sides. Count the sides on each shape. Don't forget to give a reason. You get nothing for just the answer.	*Level 3 Shape, space and measures* *This question is testing knowledge of basic polygons.* See *Collins Revision Guide KS3 Maths,* page 24
(b)	1		• The hexagon is twice as big, so it has sides of length 4 units. You should be able to enlarge shapes by a given scale factor.	
Total	**2**			

Question 2

Part	Mark	Answer	Comments	Where to find more help
(a)	1	55 m	• This is a question that expects you to read information from a diagram. Find the Bandstand and the Tennis Courts on the map and read off the distance between them.	*Level 3 Number* *This question is testing skill in reading diagrams and simple calculations.* See *Collins Revision Guide KS3 Maths,* page 1
(b)	1	Café and Kiosk	• Look on the map for a distance of 153 m.	
(c)	1	Kiosk; 24 m	• Find both places on the map. Read the distances and subtract them. Remember you can use a calculator for this.	
(d)	2	379 m	• Trace Sunhil's route round the park and add up all the distances. $153 + 92 + 55 + 79 = 379$ • You would gain 1 mark for showing the separate distances but not finding the correct total.	
Total	**5**			

Question 3

Part	Mark	Answer	Comments	Where to find more help
(a)	1	306; Three hundred and six *Or* 603; Six hundred and three	• There are two options. Both have a zero 'tens' digit so you have to be careful how you write the numbers in words.	*Level 3 Number* *This question is testing understanding of place value.*
(b)	1	630; Six hundred and thirty *Or* 360; Three hundred and sixty	• There are two options. Both have a zero 'units' digit.	See *Collins Revision Guide KS3 Maths,* page 4
(c)	1	723	• If the number is odd, it must end in 3 or 7. The biggest number it must start with the 7, so 723 is the answer.	
	1	732	• The number must end in 2, so 732 is the answer.	
Total	**4**			

Question 4

Part	Mark	Answer	Comments	Where to find more help
(a)	1	9	• Read off how many pupils scored a Level 2 from each bar chart and add them up. There were 3 in Form 6A, 4 in Form 6B and 2 in Form 6C.	*Level 4 Handling data* *This question is testing skills in reading and interpreting bar charts.*
(b)	1	22	• Add up the sizes of all the bars in form 6B: 4 + 8 + 6 + 4 = 22	
(c)	1	6C; *and* They have more pupils achieving higher National Tests levels.	• Looking at the bar charts it should be clear that Form 6C have bigger bars at the higher levels.	See *Collins Revision Guide KS3 Maths,* page 34
Total	**3**			

Question 5

Part	Mark	Answer	Comments	Where to find more help
(a)	1	5	• All polyhedra have faces, edges and vertices. A triangular prism has 5 faces, 9 edges and 6 vertices.	*Level 3 Shape, space and measures* *This question is testing recognition and understanding of the properties of 3-D shapes.*
(b)	1	8	• Vertices mean corners. A cuboid has 6 faces, 12 edges and 8 corners.	
(c)	1	6	• The shape that is left is a frustum which has a top, a base and four sides.	See *Collins Revision Guide KS3 Maths,* page 24
Total	**3**			

Question 6

Part	Mark	Answer	Comments	Where to find more help
	2	Scheme B by £1.32	• You must show your working. Scheme A costs £50 + 16 × £24.82 = £447.12. Scheme B costs 12 × £37.15 = £445.80. • You would gain 1 mark by showing the two totals for the different schemes.	*Level 3 Number and algebra* *This question is testing understanding of a formula in words and using a calculator effectively.* See *Collins Revision Guide KS3 Maths,* pages 6 and 18
Total	**2**			

THIS IS THE START OF THE TIER 4–6 PAPER

Question 7

Part	Mark	Answer	Comments	Where to find more help
(a)	1	93	• Add up all the numbers for boys: 54 + 27 + 12	*Level 4 Number and handling data* *This question is testing skills in reading information from a table.* See *Collins Revision Guide KS3 Maths,* page 34
(b)	1	72	• Find the total that said 'Yes' (54 + 63 = 117) and subtract the total that said 'No' (27 + 18 = 45). Subtract the answers: 117 − 45 = 72	
(c)	2	Yes: 36; No: 15; Don't know: 9	• This is a calculator paper so you can calculate 60% as 60 × 60 ÷ 100. The total must be 60 staff. • You would gain 1 mark if two of the answers are correct.	
(d)	1	Year 7, Year 8 and Year 9 across the top; Yes and No down the side	• A two-way table is a means of recording two facts about something in a table. The two facts are 'What year' and 'Do they want a shorter lunch'. Emily can then write a tally mark in the appropriate box on the table.	
Total	**5**			

Question 8

Part	Mark	Answer	Comments	Where to find more help
(a)	1	3	• You have to use the key to identify the correct cross on the chart. This is the one at (3, 64).	*Level 4 Handling data* *This question is testing skills in reading and understanding information from a scatter diagram.*
(b)	1	Harold Wilson	• Look along the horizontal axis for 6 years and up the vertical axis for 49 years. The nearest cross to this point is f, which represents Harold Wilson.	
(c)	1	Cross at (2.5, 58)	• Move across the horizontal axis to halfway between 2 and 3, and up to 58 on the vertical axis.	See *Collins Revision Guide KS3 Maths,* page 39
Total	**3**			

Question 9

Part	Mark	Answer	Comments	Where to find more help
	3	£11.05	• This is a question that tests if you can read information from a table. The family have 3 adults, 1 child and a senior citizen. They pay £4.35 to get to Barnsley but £6.70 to get back. You must show all your working in this type of question so you may gain some working marks even if you don't get the final answer correct. • You would gain 2 marks if you showed the total for the trip into Barnsley and the total for the trip out. • You would gain 1 mark if you found just one of these totals.	*Level 4 Number* *This question is testing identification of the information to solve a problem and finding a strategy to solve it.* See *Collins Revision Guide KS3 Maths,* page 6
Total	**3**			

Question 10

Part	Mark	Answer	Comments	Where to find more help
(a)	1	5.9 °C	• This is a decimal subtraction that you can do on a calculator.	*Level 4 Number* *This question is testing skills in working with decimals.*
(b)	1	15.5 °C	• Add 2.8 to 12.7.	
(c)	2	9.2 °F	• Multiply ⁻10.4 by 2 to give ⁻20.8. Then add 30. • You would gain 1 mark if you showed the intermediate value of ⁻20.8 °F.	See *Collins Revision Guide KS3 Maths,* page 6
Total	**4**			

Question 11

Part	Mark	Answer	Comments	Where to find more help
(a)	1	Any rectangle with a perimeter of 20 cm	• The perimeter is the distance around the shape. The total of the length and width must be 10 cm. e.g. 8 by 2, 9 by 1, 7 by 3, 6 by 4 or a 5 cm square.	*Level 4 Shape, space and measures* *This question is testing understanding of the rules for the area of a triangle.* See *Collins Revision Guide KS3 Maths,* page 29
Total	**1**			

THIS IS THE START OF THE TIER 5–7 PAPER

Question 11 continued

Part	Mark	Answer	Comments	Where to find more help
(b)	1	Another rectangle with a perimeter of 20 cm	• The answer should be different from the answer to part (a).	*Level 5 Shape, space and measures*
(c)	2	The base and height should multiply together to give 20, e.g. base 4, height 5.	• The triangle must be isosceles, i.e. symmetrical. • You would gain 1 mark for any isosceles triangle.	
Total	**3**			

Question 12

Part	Mark	Answer	Comments	Where to find more help
(a)	2	51 and 56	• The number must be one more than a multiple of 5. • You would gain 1 mark for just one of the answers.	*Level 5 Algebra* *This question is testing understanding of multiples and factors.* See *Collins Revision Guide KS3 Maths,* page 16
(b)	1	51; 51 is a multiple of 3	• The answer must be a multiple of 3, and 56 is not. You must give a reason to get the mark.	
Total	**3**			

Question 13

Part	Mark	Answer	Comments	Where to find more help
(a)	2	33% or $33\frac{1}{3}$, 35%	• The first fraction is $\frac{1}{3}$ and the second is $\frac{7}{20}$. You should know the percentage equal to a third. To convert $\frac{7}{20}$ to a percentage, multiply top and bottom by 5 to give $\frac{35}{100}$. • You would gain 1 mark for just one of the answers.	*Level 5 Number* *This question involves the equivalences between percentages, decimals and ratios.* See *Collins Revision Guide KS3 Maths*, page 54
(b)	1	$\frac{3}{8}$	• You should know that $\frac{1}{8}$ is equivalent to the decimal 0.125.	
	1	37.5%	• On your calculator you can do $3 \div 8 \times 100$.	
Total	**4**			

Question 14

Part	Mark	Answer	Comments	Where to find more help
(a)	1	$n - 4$	• There is a clue in the question with 5 more than n being $n + 5$.	*Level 5 Algebra* *This question is testing basic algebra.*
	1	$3n$	• Three times as many means $3 \times$.	
(b)	2	$6n + 1$	• Add all the number of pencils together: $n + n + 5 + n - 4 + 3n$ • You would gain 1 mark if you totalled the pencils of three of the four pupils correctly.	See *Collins Revision Guide KS3 Maths*, page 62
(c)	1	119	• Calculate: $3 \times 40 - 1 = 120 - 1$	
(d)	1	117	• Calculate: $3 \times (40 - 1) = 3 \times 39$ Work out the bracket first.	
Total	**6**			

Question 15

Part	Mark	Answer	Comments	Where to find more help
(a)	1	Asif, because his results will be biased; *or* Cassie, because the sample is not representative; *or* Cassie, because the sample is too small	• Surveys should cover a wide range of people. Asif is asking people who already use the canteen so he will not get any answers from people who do not use the canteen. Cassie will be asking people with similar habits so will not get a wide range or there may be only a few members in the hockey team.	*Level 5 Handling data* *This question tests skills in designing a questionnaire and collecting data for a survey.* See *Collins Revision Guide KS3 Maths*, page 197
(b)	1	Benjy, because he will get a wide range	• This sample will give a wide range of pupils from different backgrounds.	
Total	**2**			

Question 16

Part	Mark	Answer	Comments	Where to find more help
(a)	1	$^3/_5$	• There are 3 red counters out of a total of 5 counters. You should always give probabilities as fractions if possible.	*Level 5 Handling data* *This question is testing understanding of probability.* See *Collins Revision Guide KS3 Maths,* page 89
(b)	1	1 red, 3 blue	• Any combination where the ratio of the red : blue is 1 : 3, e.g. 2 red and 6 blue.	
Total	**2**			

Question 17

Part	Mark	Answer	Comments	Where to find more help
	2	FB = 5 cm $q = 120°$ $p = 60°$	• The two trapeziums form a regular hexagon, which has an interior angle of 120°. p is half of q. • You would gain 1 mark if you had two correct answers.	*Level 5 Shape, space and measures* *This question is testing understanding of the properties of regular polygons.* See *Collins Revision Guide KS3 Maths,* page 72
Total	**2**			

Question 18

Part	Mark	Answer	Comments	Where to find more help
(a)	2	37	• The calculation is 4500 ÷ 120 = 37.5. You have to convert 4.5 litres to 4500 ml. The answer must be rounded down as only complete plants can be counted. • You would gain 1 mark by showing the correct calculation but giving the answer as 37.5 or 38.	*Level 5 Shape, space and measures* *This question tests conversion between metric units and interpreting a decimal answer.* See *Collins Revision Guide KS3 Maths,* page 74
(b)	1	2.925 kg	• Calculate 45% of 6.5 kg. The easiest way to do this is to use a multiplier: 0.45×6.5 • As this is an estimate, an answer of 2.9 is acceptable.	
Total	**3**			

THIS IS THE END OF THE TIER 3–5 PAPER

> ## THIS IS THE START OF THE TIER 6–8 PAPER

Question 19

Part	Mark	Answer	Comments	Where to find more help
(a)	1	11:9	• The ratio is 22:18, which can be cancelled by 2.	*Level 6 Number*
(b)	1	1:1	• After 5 days both plants are the same height.	*This question tests understanding of ratio.*
(c)	1	Yes. The day before they were measured the heights were 18:12.	• Instead of working the heights forward, you have to work them backwards.	See *Collins Revision Guide KS3 Maths*, page 106
Total	**3**			

Question 20

Part	Mark	Answer	Comments	Where to find more help
(a)	1 1	$48\,\text{cm}^2$; $54\,\text{cm}^2$	• Calculate the areas as rectangles and triangles.	*Level 6 Shape, space and measures*
(b)	2	Greater; the volume is $18\,\text{cm}^3$	• You find the volume by calculating: area of cross section × length The area of a triangular face is $3\,\text{cm}^2$. • You would gain 1 mark for using the volume formula with the cross-sectional area as $3\,\text{cm}^2$.	*This question involves volumes of basic shapes and understanding nets.* See *Collins Revision Guide KS3 Maths*, page 139
Total	**4**			

Question 21

Part	Mark	Answer	Comments	Where to find more help
(a)	2	Trees 63.36; Grass 29.04; Shrub 39.6	• You need to calculate 48% of 132, and so on. • You would gain 1 mark for two correct answers out of three.	*Level 6 Number and Handling data*
(b)	2	Grass 3.328; Shrub 1.352	• If 0.52 acres is 10% then the whole estate covers 5.2 acres. • You would gain 1 mark for one correct answer out of two.	*This question tests skills in reading pie charts and evaluating percentages.* See *Collins Revision Guide KS3 Maths*, page 147

Part	Mark	Answer	Comments	Where to find more help
(c)	1	The estate has less trees but more grass as a proportion of the land area.	• The question asks you to compare proportions not amounts. A proportion is the percentage of land of each type. So, even though the estate is much smaller than the woodland, it still has a greater proportion of grassland.	
Total	**5**			

Question 22

Part	Mark	Answer	Comments	Where to find more help
(a)	1	28.8	• Cross multiply to give $144 = 5x$.	*Level 6 Algebra*
(b)	1	7.5	• Cross multiply to give $12y = 90$.	*This question tests skills in solving linear equations.* See *Collins Revision Guide KS3 Maths,* page 117
Total	**2**			

Question 23

Part	Mark	Answer	Comments	Where to find more help
(a)	1	45°	• All of the angles at the centre are equal. There are 8 angles giving $360 \div 8 = 45°$.	*Level 7 Shape, space and measures*
(b)	2	68°	• Angle x is the exterior angle of a triangle which is equal to the sum of the two opposite interior angles. Alternatively, you can work out the angle next to x as 112° using angles in a triangle. • You would gain 1 mark if you showed the value 112°.	*This question tests understanding of angle properties of triangles and regular polygons.* See *Collins Revision Guide KS3 Maths,* page 132
Total	**3**			

Question 24

Part	Mark	Answer	Comments	Where to find more help
	2	A : C : B	• Circle B has an area of $\pi \times 20^2 = 1256 \, \text{cm}^2$. • Circle C has a radius of $20 \div 2\pi = 3.318$. The area is $\pi \times 3.318^2 = 31.8 \, \text{cm}^2$ • You would gain 1 mark if you showed in your working the areas of at least two circles.	*Level 6 Shape, space and measures* ***This question tests calculation of areas of circles using the formula $A = \pi r^2$.*** See *Collins Revision Guide KS3 Maths,* page 139
Total	**2**			

THIS IS THE END OF THE TIER 4–6 PAPER

Question 25

Part	Mark	Answer	Comments	Where to find more help
(a)	1	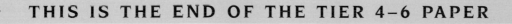	• The first diagram needs 1 octagon and 2 squares.	*Level 7 Shape, space and measures and Algebra* ***This question tests recognition of shapes and clear explanation of methods.*** See *Collins Revision Guide KS3 Maths,* page 172
	1		• The second diagram needs 2 octagons and 2 squares.	
(b)	1	Shape A can be split into an octagon and 4 triangles which make a square.	• You could show this with a diagram.	
	1	Shape $B = T - S$	• Shape B has the 4 triangles taken away from the octagon.	

Part	Mark	Answer	Comments	Where to find more help
(c)	2	$T - S = \frac{5}{9}(S + T)$ So $9T - 9S = 5S + 5T$ $\quad\quad 4T = 14S$ giving $\quad S = \frac{4}{14}T$ which cancels to the correct answer.	• Alternatively, S covers four half squares and T covers 14 half squares. This gives $S = \frac{4}{14}T$, which cancels to the correct answer.	
Total	**6**			

Question 26

Part	Mark	Answer	Comments	Where to find more help
(a)	3	15 days	• The plant has to grow $100 - 3.5 = 96.5$ cm. At 6.5 cm per day this will take $96.5 \div 6.5 = 14.84$ days, which is about 15 days. • You will gain 2 marks for showing 14.84. You will gain 1 mark for showing 96.5 and dividing this by 6.5.	*Level 7 Number* *This question tests skills in interpreting information and devising a strategy to solve a complex problem.* See *Collins Revision Guide KS3 Maths,* page 164
(b)	1	80	• Add up the frequencies.	
(c)	2	14.5	• Multiply the number of seeds by the frequencies and add them together. Then divide by 80. • Answer is 14.5375 but this is rounded off. • You would gain 1 mark if your working shows 1163 total seeds.	
(d)	3	170 000	• There are approximately $14.5375 \times 20\,000$ seeds. Work out 60% of this as 174 450. Then round the answer to 2 significant figures. • You would gain 1 mark for showing $14.5 \times 20\,000 = 290\,000$, and 1 mark for 174 000 or 174 450.	
Total	**9**			

Question 27

Part	Mark	Answer	Comments	Where to find more help
(a)	1	1.5	• Picture A is 3 cm wide. Picture B is 4.5 cm wide. $4.5 \div 3 = 1.5$	*Level 7 Shape, space and measures* *This question is about similar and congruent figures.* See *Collins Revision Guide KS3 Maths,* page 192
Total	**1**			

THIS IS THE END OF THE TIER 5–7 PAPER

Question 27 continued

Part	Mark	Answer	Comments	Where to find more help
(b)	1	$-\frac{1}{2}$	• Picture C is half the size of picture A and is turned upside down which is why it a negative scale factor.	*Level 8 Shape, space and measures*
(c)	1	The sides have not increased in the same ratio.	• The heights of pictures A and B are the the same, but the width has increased by a factor of 1.5.	
(d)	1	7.5 cm	• The scale factor is $9.5 \div 3.8 = 2.5$, so the height of D is 3×2.5.	
Total	**3**			

Question 28

Part	Mark	Answer	Comments	Where to find more help
(a)	2	13p	• If 6p represents 14% then the total cost of the banana is $6 \div 0.14 = 42.85$, so the banana costs 43p. • You would gain 1 mark for showing a correct calculation.	*Level 8 Number* *This is a problem on reverse percentages.* See *Collins Revision Guide KS3 Maths,* page 212, question 3
(b)	2	37.5%	• A 15% reduction in the supermarkets share is 2.25 pence. This means the grower gets 8.25. This is a $2.25 \div 6 \times 100 = 37.5\%$ increase. • You would gain 1 mark for showing a correct calculation.	
Total	**4**			

Question 29

Part	Mark	Answer	Comments	Where to find more help
(a)	1	1.708 696 245	• You should be able to use your calculator efficiently. You should use brackets to make sure you enter the calculation correctly.	*Level 8 Number* *This is a question on using a calculator efficiently.* See *Collins Revision Guide KS3 Maths,* page 212, question 5
(b)	1	1.71		
Total	**2**			

Question 30

Part	Mark	Answer	Comments	Where to find more help
(a)	1	United States	• First find the highest power of 10 (in this case 8) and then the largest initial number.	*Level 8 Number* *This is a question on standard form.* See *Collins Revision Guide KS3 Maths,* page 211, question 1
(b)	2	7.4281×10^{11}	• You should know how to use your calculator to enter standard form numbers. This is usually the key marked EE or EXP. • You would gain 1 mark for the digits 74281.	
Total	**3**			

Question 31

Part	Mark	Answer	Comments	Where to find more help
(a)	2	12.6 cm	• Use Pythagoras theorem: $BC^2 = \sqrt{14^2 - 6^2}$ • You would gain 1 mark for showing the calculation.	*Level 8 Shape, space and measures* *This question is about Pythagoras and trigonometry.* See *Collins Revision Guide KS3 Maths,* page 217, question 15
(b)	2	35°	• This is a trigonometric problem. To calculate the angle use $\tan^{-1}(14 \div 20)$. • You would gain 1 mark for showing the calculation.	
Total	**4**			

Question 32

Part	Mark	Answer	Comments	Where to find more help
(a)	1	$x^2 - 2x - 3$	• Expand this by FOIL or by expanding each bracket: $x(x - 3) + 1(x - 3)$	*Level 8 Algebra* *This question tests skills in expanding brackets and factorising.* See *Collins Revision Guide KS3 Maths,* page 214, question 9
(b)	1	$4x^2$	• Don't forget to square 2 as well as x.	
(c)	1	$(2x - 3)(2x + 3)$	• This is the difference of two squares, which you should recognise.	
Total	**3**			

Question 33

Part	Mark	Answer	Comments	Where to find more help
	3	3.75 cm	• The volume of a cylinder is $\pi r^2 h$, so $\pi r^2 \times 16 = 225 \times \pi$. So $r^2 = 14.0625$ • You would gain 1 mark for the formula and 1 mark for $r^2 = 14.0625$	*Level 8 Shape, space and measures* *This question tests skills in rearranging formulae.* See *Collins Revision Guide KS3 Maths,* page 212, question 6
Total	**3**			

Question 34

Part	Mark	Answer	Comments	Where to find more help
	3	$x = £4.75$ $y = £2.50$	• The two equations are $2x + 3y = 17$ and $3x + y = 16.75$. Multiply the second by 3 to give $9x + 3y = 50.25$. Subtract the first to give $7x = 33.25$ which gives $x = 4.75$. Then substitute back to find y. • You would gain 1 mark for setting up the equations and 1 mark for eliminating one variable.	*Level 8 Algebra* *This question tests skills in solving simultaneous equations.* See *Collins Revision Guide KS3 Maths,* page 214, question 8
Total	**3**			

THIS IS THE END OF THE TIER 6–8 PAPER

Mental arithmetic tests

Mental arithmetic test C (Tiers 3–5)

Each question is worth 1 mark only.

Number	Answer	Comments	*Collins Revision Guide KS3 Maths*
1	207	Two hundred and seven does not have a 'tens' number in it so the second digit is zero.	Place value, page 4
2	5 up to 10 × 10.	You need to know your multiplication tables	Multiplication tables, page 1
3	£500	You should be able to round to the nearest 10, 100 or 1000.	Rounding, page 60
4	35	Think of this as 'a number minus 10 equals twenty five'.	Solving equations, page 18
5	£10	Twenty-five per cent is a quarter. A quarter of £40 is easy to work out.	Fractions and, percentages, page 8
6	72	You need to know your tables.	Multiplication tables, page 1
7	e.g. 0.75	Any number between a half and one will do. You can write your answer as a fraction.	Decimals and fractions, page 8
8	⁻5	Think of this as ⁻7 + 2.	Directed numbers, page 50
9	$x - 3$	If this was a number problem you would have, for example, $7 - 3$. Just replace the number by the letter.	Basic algebra, page 62
10	23:00 hours	Count two and a half hours back from one thirty.	
11	5.2, 5.5	You should be able to do calculation such as 4.9 + 0.3 mentally.	Decimals, page 6
12	£6.78	This is 700 − 22, then convert to pounds.	Decimals, page 6
13		There are 12 squares. 12 ÷ 3 = 4. Any four squares will do.	Fractions, page 8
14	120	The 'trick' is to add the units (3 + 7) to give 10, so the problem is 50 + 60 + 10.	
15	90°	Perpendicular means 'at right angles'.	Basic geometry, page 70
16	55–65 families	The two bars in total are 100, so the bar for Spain is about 60.	Bar charts, page 34
17	Volume or capacity	You need to know the basic units and what they represent.	Metric units, page 74
18	£2.10	Do this in parts: £6 ÷ 3 = £2, 30p ÷ 3 = 10p	
19	10 km	The calculation is: 4 × 2.5	
20	75 pupils	If 25% is 50 then there are 150 pupils who like Maths and Science. Half of these like Maths.	Pie charts, page 86
21	300 000	There are five zeros in one hundred thousand.	Place value, page 4
22	15	There are about two and a half centimetres in an inch.	Imperial units, page 74
23	92 or 96	Multiples of 4 are numbers in the 4-times table. 100 is a multiple of 4, so subtract 4 from 100 to give a number in range.	Multiples, page 16

Number	Answer	Comments	Collins Revision Guide KS3 Maths
24	105–120 degrees	The angle is bigger than 90°. The actual answer is 114°.	Angles, page 70
25	$5a$	Just work out the numbers in front of a, i.e. $6 + 2 - 3 = 5$.	Basic algebra, page 18
26	14:33 and 14:54	Use the complete timetables to work out how long each part of the journey takes. Barnsley to Silkstone is 10 minutes and Silkstone to Denby is 21 minutes.	
27	66	Combine together numbers that add to give multiples of 10, i.e. $14 + 16 = 30$, $8 + 12 = 20$. That leaves $10 + 6 = 16$. $20 + 30 + 16 = 66$	Multiples, page 16
28		The top and one side are missing. There are other ways the net could be drawn but this is the most straightforward.	2-D and 3-D shapes, page 24
29	2 red marbles	If there are two red marbles, that makes ten in the bag altogether. So P(red) is 2 out of 10.	Probability, page 89
30	312	The numbers are half of those given, so the answer need to be 'halved' twice or divided by 4.	

Mental arithmetic test A/B (Tiers 4-6, 5-7, 6-8)

Each question is worth 1 mark only.

Number	Answer	Comments	Collins Revision Guide KS3 Maths
1	5400	Multiplying whole numbers by 100 means adding two zeros to the end.	Multiplying by 100, page 4
2	1000 m	You should know the relationship between metric units.	Metric units, page 74
3	16	You can do this by $30 \div 3 + 18 \div 3$.	Simple fractions, page 8
4	$^-10$	Think of this as $^-6 - 4$.	Negative numbers, page 50
5	7	This is the square root of 49. You could also give the answer $^-7$.	Simple formulae, page 62
6	3.75	Think of this as $5 \div 2 + 2.5 \div 2$.	Decimals, page 48
7	8.5 kg	The mass could be within half a kilogram of the given value.	Accuracy of measurement, page 189
8	5 months	Imagine (or draw) a line across at 20. There are five dots above this.	Line graphs, page 39
9	Isosceles triangle	The shape is:	Symmetry of 2-D shapes, page 72
10		The first number in a coordinate is the 'across' number and the second number is the 'up' number.	Coordinates, page 19

Number	Answer	Comments	*Collins Revision Guide KS3 Maths*
11	20	This is $2 \div 0.1 = 20 \div 1$. Move the decimal point in each number to keep the value of the calculation the same.	Working with decimals, page 97
12	16	You should know that 5 miles ≈ 8 kilometres.	Conversion factors, page 75
13	1 : 1.5	Divide the second number in the ratio by the first number.	Ratio, page 106
14	75 pupils	If 25% is 50 then there are 150 pupils who like Maths and Science. Half of these like Maths.	Pie charts, page 86
15	90°	Perpendicular means 'at right angles'.	Basic geometry, page 70
16	7	If $3x - 1 = 20$ then $3x = 21$, so $x = 7$.	Linear equations, page 117
17	55 cm	10% of 50 is 5. Add this on to 50.	Percentages, page 104
18	1 m^3	Remember to convert 50 cm to 0.5 m. The volume is $2 \times 1 \times 0.5 \text{ m}^3$.	Volume of a cuboid, page 141
19	10	Two-thirds of 60 is 40. A quarter of 40 is 10.	Fractions, page 53
20	3, 4, 5, 6, 7	The inequalities mean that 3 is included, but 8 is not. Integers are whole numbers.	Inequalities, page 176
21	3	The factors of 24 are: 1, 3, 4, 6, 8, 12, 24.	Factors, page 16
22	99	The rule is $2 \times$ position $- 1$. So the 50th odd number is $2 \times 50 - 1 = 99$.	Finding the nth term, page 114
23		The line goes through all the, points whose coordinates add up to 5, e.g. (0, 5), (1, 4), (2, 3), (3, 2), (4, 1), (5, 0).	Drawing linear graphs, page 123
24	60–64 cm	The formula for the circumference is $2\pi r = 2 \times 10 \times 3.14 = 62.8$.	Circumference of a circle, page 139
25	495	The largest number is 651. The smallest is 156. The difference is $651 - 156$.	Four operations on number, page 1
26	160	The approximation is $20 \times 40 \div 5$. 5 goes into 20 four times. $4 \times 40 = 160$	Estimating, page 158
27	$3y + 1$	Think of what is needed to make the original term, or divide by what is in the brackets, i.e. $6xy^2 = 2xy \times 3y$ and $2xy = 2xy \times 1$.	Factorisation, page 215
28	6	A tetrahedron is a triangular-based pyramid.	3-D shapes, page 25
29	3 red marbles	If there are 3 red marbles, the total number of marbles is 15, so the probability of red is 3 out of 15 which cancels down to one-fifth.	Probabilities, page 89
30	22	Quickly count: 100, 101–109, 110–190 and 200, which is $2 + 9 + 9 + 2$.	

Key Stage 3 Mathematics
Mental Arithmetic Test C
(Tiers 3–5)

First Name ....

Last Name ....

School ....

Pupil Number | | | | | |

Total Marks

Time: 5 seconds

1

1

2

2

3 £   £489.95

3

4 $p - q = 25$

4

5 £   25%

5

6

6

7

7

0   −7

8

9   *x*

0

Time: 10 seconds

10   1:30 am

10

11 4.3, 4 6, 4.9, ... , ...

11

12 £   22p

12

13

13

14   63   57

14

15

15

16

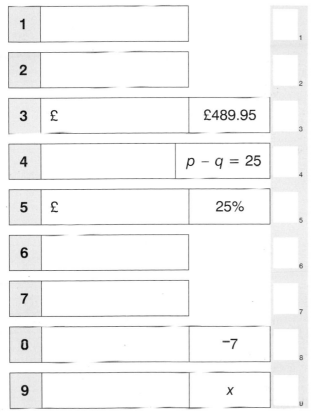

France   Spain

families

16

17

17

18 £   £6.30

18

19

B

4 cm

A

km

19

20

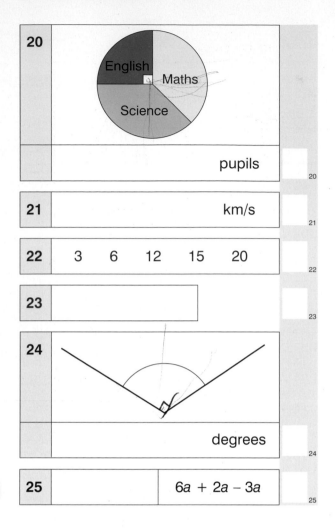

English Maths Science

pupils 20

21 km/s 21

22 3 6 12 15 20 22

23 23

24 degrees 24

25 $6a + 2a - 3a$ 25

Time: 15 seconds

26

Barnsley	11:05	12:58	14:23
Silkstone	11:15	13:08	....
Denby	11:36	13:29	....

26

27 6 8 10 12 14 16 27

28

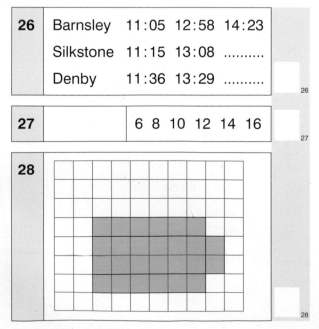

28

29 Black   8 marbles

Red .... marbles

$P(\text{red}) = \frac{1}{5}$

red marbles 29

30 $24 \times 52 = 1248$
12×26 30

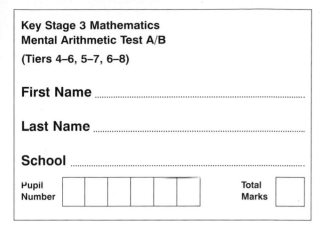

Key Stage 3 Mathematics
Mental Arithmetic Test A/B
(Tiers 4–6, 5–7, 6–8)

First Name ....

Last Name ....

School ....

Pupil Number							Total Marks	

Time: 5 seconds

1		54	1
2		m	2
3			3
4		−6	4
5		$y = x^2$	5
6		7.5	6
7		kg	7

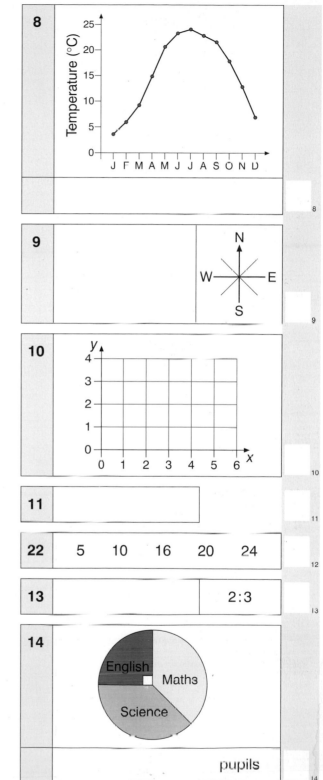

Time: 10 seconds

8

9

10

11		11

22	5 10 16 20 24	12

13		2:3	13

14

pupils

15	

16		$3x - 1 = 20$

17		cm

18		m^3

19	

20		$3 \le n < 8$

Time: 15 seconds

21	

22	

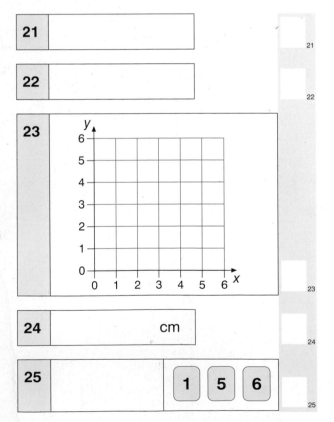

24		cm

25		1 5 6

26		$\dfrac{19.8 \times 42.6}{5.21}$

27	$6xy^2 + 2xy = 2xy(\ldots\ldots + \ldots\ldots)$

28	

29	Black 8 marbles
	White 4 marbles
	Red .... marbles
	P(red) = $\dfrac{1}{5}$
	red marbles

30	